Cathedrals in Britain

Gerald Randall

with line drawings by
Ed Perera

 Letts**Guides**

Charles Letts & Co Ltd
London, Edinburgh, München
& New York

First published 1979
by Charles Letts & Co Ltd
Diary House, Borough Road, London SE1 1DW

Edited by Stuart Laing and Kay McCann

ISBN 0 85097 279 5

Printed in Great Britain by
Letts Erskine Ltd, Dalkeith

Contents

Acknowledgements

We are indebted to the publishers of the Pitkin
Pride of Britain series for permission to use their
illustrations as reference material in the
preparation of the line illustrations and
cathedral ground plans which appear on pages:
5, 6, 9-11, 13, 16, 33, 34, 36-38, 42, 43, 45, 46,
48, 50, 53, 56-63, 65, 67, 69, 70, 72-74, 78-83,
85-88, 90-95, 97-99, 101-106, 108, 110, 111, 115,
117-119, 121, 123, 125, 126, 128, 129, 131-133.

We are grateful to the following for the use of
photographs:
A. F. Kersting, London, p. 48.
British Tourist Authority, pp. 15, 17 (top), 39,
49, 55, 66, 68, 76, 112, 114, 127, 136.
Colour Library International, p. 17 (bottom).
Sonia Halliday Photographs, 19, 23, 27
(bottom).

Woodmansterne, pp. 18, 20, 21, 22, 24-27 (top),
28-32 and cover.

athedral history

A cathedral is any church, irrespective of size, which contains the throne of a bishop; it is the mother church of a diocese.

Bishops, Deans and Canons

In Britain medieval dioceses were large, and the bishops who ruled them, who alone could confirm and ordain, had to travel from manor to manor like secular feudal lords. They were also frequently great officers of state. Thus, although they often initiated and contributed generously to building schemes, they rarely present at cathedral services except on major festivals.

The cathedral, indeed, was not the bishop's property, but belonged, as it still usually does, to the dean and the chapter of resident canons, and, on appointment, the bishop has to knock on the door with his crozier to request entry. The dean and chapter are still responsible for the daily round of services, controlling the use of the building for other purposes, maintaining the fabric, and providing for visitors.

During the Middle Ages some cathedrals were attached to monasteries, and in such cases the bishop acted as abbot, while the prior, in addition to his monastic duties, acted as dean.

Cathedrals in the Middle Ages

The large scale of most cathedrals was not just a matter of prestige. Altars had to be provided so that every resident priest could say his daily Mass, and custom forbade the use of the same altar twice on the same day; a choir had to be provided for the performance of the daily offices; there had to be processional ways for great festivals and solemn occasions like the installation of a new bishop; and in those cathedrals which contained the shrine of a saint, provision had to be made for the streams of pilgrims. Consequently, a cathedral, for all its size and opulence, was essentially a working building.

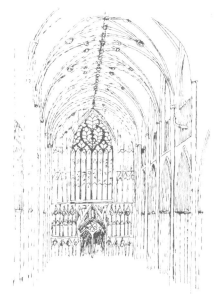

York-nave

The Reformation

In England and Wales the Dissolution of the Monasteries meant that all cathedrals became secular foundations with deans and chapters. The choir services still took place, but only twice a day, and in English instead of Latin. The nave held its place for congregational worship, and the importance of the pulpit increased with the Protestant emphasis on preaching. But much of the structure became redundant, and it is a matter for deep gratitude that deans and chapters nevertheless maintained them in an age when medieval architecture was generally despised.

Scottish cathedrals were less fortunate. When episcopacy was abolished, and there was no longer a function for them to fulfil, most of them fell wholly or partially into ruin. A few have since been restored, but only two, Glasgow and Kirkwall, both now parish churches, have always remained intact.

Cathedrals today

While the historic cathedrals of England and Wales have never been more effective mother churches than they are today, they are no longer just places of worship. Chapters recognise that the majority of visitors are cultural rather than religious pilgrims, and a cathedral's calendar of events will usually include plays, concerts, and choral festivals alongside the standard services and celebrations. The Three Choirs Festival, for example, run by Gloucester, Hereford, and Worcester, is the oldest festival of its kind in the world.

Historic traditions, however, are not forgotten. The English cathedral choir, with its magnificent repertoire, regularly sings evensong and no day ever goes by without some act of worship taking place. The cathedrals are still patrons of the arts and crafts too: stonemasons, carpenters, and glaziers trained in the old traditions are still needed to keep the fabrics in good repair. The best places to find modern furnishings in the great tradition are Coventry and Liverpool (RC), closely followed by Chichester and Llandaff.

The Chapel of Industry, Coventry Cathedral

athedral building

Design and layout

While no two are identical in plan, there is a broad similarity about all the cathedrals of Britain up to and including Coventry. The function of each part is best understood in medieval terms.

Usually the building is in the shape of a Latin cross, with the place where the east-west axis and the shorter north-south arm meet being called, logically enough, the *crossing*.

The area of the crossing at the heart of the building contained the bishop's *choir*, where the daily offices were sung. The present-day choir has usually been shifted eastwards so that it is all in the chancel. To its east is the high altar for the principal celebration of Mass, in the part called the *presbytery*, or priests' area. The choir east of the crossing and the presbytery, together with the side aisles, form the *chancel*. Further east, the *retro-choir* often contained the shrine of a saint, though in early times the shrine lay immediately below the high altar in a *crypt*. The *chancel aisles* lead to a wide space in the retrochoir called the *ambulatory*. The *Lady Chapel*, dedicated to the Virgin Mary, was usually, though not always, to be found at the extreme east of the building.

The main *transept*, often aisled, runs north and south across the building. Its primary purpose was to provide extra altar space, and the division into separate chapels is often preserved. A secondary, but by no means negligible purpose was to provide abutment for the *crossing tower* – usually the main vertical accent of the cathedral's exterior.

The *nave* was the people's part of the church. It rarely contained seating, except perhaps for stone benches along the side walls, but was often of vast size. Congregations stood, knelt, or walked about during services as they do in Eastern Orthodox churches today. It acted as a sort of civic hall for all kinds of secular activities too – even occasionally as a market place. The *aisles*, always vaulted, as were the chancel and transept aisles, formed processional ways, but were primarily to form an abutment for the main structure, especially necessary if it carried a high vault.

Unless there was a separate detached belfry, *western towers* often housed the bells, for crossing towers were rarely stable enough to withstand the stresses set up by a peal.

Chapels could be added almost anywhere. Sometimes they were attached to western towers; sometimes they were set up against nave piers; but more often, additional chapels occur east of the crossing. Some were chantries, endowed by individuals, or, more rarely in cathedrals, gilds, for the purpose of providing Masses for the dead then commemorated. All chantries were dissolved at the Reformation, but their architecture often survives together with the tombs within them.

Somewhere in the eastern parts, too, there would be a *vestry*, where clergy robed, and a *sacristy*, where the plate and altar linen were kept.

Finally, every cathedral, whether monastic or secular, needed a *chapter house* where daily business would be conducted. Most, too, had *cloisters*, an integral part of every monastery, but usual too in secular cathedrals where they gave access to such places as libraries and song schools. In place of monastic buildings, secular cathedrals had *precincts*, where the houses and offices of the cathedral officials stood.

Saxon architecture

Since no Saxon cathedral survives except for the ruins of North Elmham, the foundations of Winchester, and the crypt of Ripon, little need be said about them. They were comparatively small, but often, like medieval cathedrals, the products of several centuries of growth and change.

Norman architecture

Soon after the Norman Conquest, every English cathedral was rebuilt on a vastly greater scale. Norman Winchester, for example, was five times the size of Saxon Winchester; Norwich was ten times the size of North Elmham; and there is no reason to think that these were unusual. Norman architecture actually reached England before the Conquest, in Edward the Confessor's Westminster Abbey. It was introduced into Wales and Scotland early in the twelfth century.

Apart from being extremely long, dark, ponderous buildings, the chief characteristics of Norman cathedrals were as follows:

Arches were round.

Piers were either compound (that is, with a large core with a variety of shafts or demi-shafts attached to it) or they were cylindrical. The massive girth of these piers gives a false impression of strength, since they were mostly filled with rubble.

The arcade, gallery, and clerestory, the three storeys of the elevation, were comparable in height – except in one or two places like the nave of Gloucester. A ratio of about 6:5:4 would be about average.

Roofs were steeply pitched, and towers always carried pyramid roofs or spires – though no original Norman spire survives.

Capitals were usually simple cushions, often in later work divided into scallops. Moulded and Corinthianesque capitals occur occasionally.

Ornament was varied, but generally shallowly carved – with a hand-axe rather than a chisel. Zig-zag is the commonest form.

Norman architecture was superseded gradually between about 1170 and 1200.

Gothic architecture

Gothic was a term of abuse invented by seventeenth-century aesthetes who affected everything Italian, but it was retained as a term of affection as medieval architecture came to be appreciated again. It was invented in France, and the east end of Canterbury Cathedral is an example of early French Gothic built in England. Most of

Wells and the choir of Lincoln are early examples of English Gothic, which, again, preceded the introduction of the style into Wales and Scotland. The classic ingredients of Gothic are: pointed arches, used consistently throughout; rib-vaults; and flying buttresses. All these are constructional improvements.

Pointed arches are stronger than round-headed ones; rib-vaults are lighter than solid tunnel or groined vaults; and flying buttresses help to carry the thrust of vaults. Consequently there could be more and larger voids in relation to stretches of solid wall, and the whole structure became lighter. Piers became narrower in girth and better built. Towers and spires became taller.

It is usual to divide English Gothic into three phases: Early English, Decorated, and Perpendicular. Although these are useful terms, particularly in parish churches where few dates are known, their use in this book has been kept to a minimum because there is so much overlap and transition that one would have to continually qualify them. Dates for cathedral work are often known, and far more can be understood by comparing work at one cathedral with work at another than by using vague labels which tend to obscure the continuous process of experiment and development which took place throughout the Gothic period.

Some of the main guidelines to development are as follows:

Windows: Lancets without tracery are universal in the earliest Gothic. Plate tracery (that is, twin lancets with a pierced panel over and between the arch heads) appeared about 1200. Then, in the 1240s, bar tracery, another French invention, first appeared in England. The earliest bar tracery comprised a variety of geometrical patterns. Reticulated (net-like) tracery was introduced in the first years of the fourteenth century. Flowing tracery, with sinuous curves and rich designs, was in vogue from about 1330 to about 1370. In the late 1330s a rival appeared in the form of panel tracery – in which some at least of the tracery motifs have straight vertical sides, and the vertical bars between the lancets of the window stretch up as mullions to the head of the containing arch.

Vaults: Rib-vaults were invented at Durham in Norman times. Tiercerons were introduced first at Lincoln, and later developed – to present a palm-like effect – at Exeter (around 1300). Liernes first appear just after 1300 as well, and fan-vaults follow about 1360, while pendant vaults were briefly fashionable around 1500. All these forms of vault are English inventions, though ribs appeared on a smaller scale in Lombardy at about the same time as they were used at Durham.

Arches: Window arches tend to be sharper and steeper in early medieval work, though this is not true of the earliest arcades, where the round arch was still remembered. Arches drawn from four centres rather than two, and which are consequently flatter in appearance, are a late form.

Piers: These are always shafted in early work – often with Purbeck marble. Shaft rings were frequently used to fix them to the core. Later piers are more often moulded, and the shafts – which are fewer – tend to merge with the surface.

Capitals: Stiff-leaf capitals (that is, capitals with deeply cut stylized leaves) are early pieces of decoration. Later leaf-carving was more naturalistic. Still later capitals are usually plainly moulded without foliage, and frequently absent from all but the main shafts of piers.

Ornament: The most typical early Gothic ornament is dogtooth – little raised pyramids with the middle of each side cut away. Ballflower, a three-petalled flower enclosing a small ball, is characteristic ornamentation of around 1300. Later, come fleurons – flatter, stylized flowers.

Gothic died hard in Britain. It survived the Reformation, and a case can be made out for saying that Gothic survival lasted until Gothic revival began in the second half of the eighteenth century. Although after the Reformation there was a long period when Gothic was too unfashionable for use in cathedrals, and the various Renaissance and post-Renaissance styles were used instead, it

was not a time of cathedral building in Britain. The one magnificent exception is London's St Paul's. Birmingham, designed in 1709, and Derby, 1723, were both built as parish churches.

Modern architecture

The Gothic style survived until so recently as the new Anglican cathedral in Liverpool, designed admittedly as early as 1904, and Guildford, 1932. Coventry marks a transition from the Gothic idea of a cathedral to a contemporary one.

The two really contemporary cathedrals of note to date are both Roman Catholic: Liverpool and Clifton (see pp 81 and 139).

Materials

Stone is the basic material of every historic cathedral up to and including Coventry. It varies enormously in quality and appearance. The best is *oolitic limestone,* found in a band across England from Yorkshire to Dorset, and again in France – from where Caen stone was frequently imported, especially in Norman times. Oolitic limestone varies in colour from creamy-grey to golden brown. It weathers well and carves beautifully. Among cathedrals built of it are Wells, Salisbury, Ely, and Lincoln.

The inverted strainer arches of Wells Cathedral

Sandstones are variable, being usually warmer in appearance, but on the whole inferior in durability to limestone. The reason why Hereford, Worcester, and Chester are disappointing in texture outside is that the sandstone weathered so badly that it had to be replaced. At the other extreme *granite* is an intractably hard stone, indestructible, but difficult to cut and carve. It was used at Aberdeen. *Flint* was used as a last resort where no building stone could be easily obtained, as at St Albans.

True *marble* is very rare in Britain, and very little was imported in medieval times, though a good deal came in later, especially for funerary monuments. Medieval masters made do with the native substitute, shelly limestones which take a polish. The most famous quarry was at Purbeck, Dorset; other false marbles were found at Frosterley, Co. Durham, Alwalton, near Peterborough, and Bethersden, Kent. Derbyshire *alabaster* was used in the later Middle Ages when delicate carving was needed, especially for effigies and small sculptured panels.

Brick was rarely used, and always disguised, even when it became fashionable for domestic building in eastern England in the late Middle Ages. The Roman brick reused at St Albans was originally plastered outside as it still is inside. The first time brick was intended to be seen in a major cathedral was at Westminster in 1895.

Tiles were generally used for flooring; usually glazed, and often patterned.

Timber is almost as important as stone. All roofs were constructed in timber until modern times, whether open to view or hidden by stone vaults. So were many furnishings, stalls in particular, and those screens which were not made of stone. Oak was the commonest wood used for structural work and furnishing. The master carpenter ranked second only to the master mason in the cathedral building hierarchy.

Roofs and timber spires could be clad in a variety of materials including *tiles, lead, copper sheeting, shingles* (oak tiles), *stone slabs, slate* in recent times, and in medieval times occasionally even *thatch*.

Concrete has only been used this century, especially in the second half. In conjunction with *steel* it has enabled many structural innovations to be made. What it will look like as time goes on remains to be seen.

Metalwork was once more common than it is now; most medieval work in precious or even valuable metal like bronze – unless it was used for effigies – has been pillaged. Wrought-iron screens occur occasionally – both medieval, and, in St Paul's, magnificent late seventeenth-century work. Victorian metalwork was for the most part indifferent.

An idea of what was lost at the Reformation can be gained by looking at the fifteenth-century candelabra in Bristol Cathedral, and the Gloucester candlestick, made early in the twelfth century of gilded bell-metal and now in the Victoria and Albert Museum. Some very early metalwork in the form of small portable reliquaries has survived, especially in Scotland, where, for example, the Monymusk reliquary may be

Lincoln Cathedral   blank arcading

seen in the National Museum of Antiquities in Edinburgh. The best of these shrines, however, were Irish.

Furnishings

The essential furniture in a medieval church or a modern Catholic one is an *altar*, or, in a reformed church, a *holy table*, for the celebration of the Eucharist. Each altar had behind it a *reredos* or *retable* in medieval times, of stone, of wood, or merely painted on the wall. For the celebrant and his assistants to sit during parts of the liturgy, canopied seats called *sedilia* were provided, usually to the south of the high altar, and near by there was normally a *piscina*, a drain which carried away the water used to wash the communion vessels and the celebrant's hands.

Cathedrals, like monasteries and collegiate churches, always contained *stalls* for the resident clergy, and, of course, there was always a bishop's *throne* in addition. If there was a shrine, there would be a *watching loft* so that a vigil could be constantly kept on it, and an eye kept on the behaviour of pilgrims.

The choir would be divided from the nave, or at least the greater part of it, by a screen, usually of stone, called the *pulpitum*.

Various other *screens* would partition off chapels and divide the choir from the chancel aisles. Screens often had lofts with parapets. The organ might stand on the pulpitum, and preaching was sometimes conducted from the pulpitum loft. Later it became the custom to provide a separate pulpit, and this custom became universal after the Reformation when most lofts were destroyed. There would probably be a *lectern*, or reading desk in the choir, possibly of stone, but more probably of brass or wood. A *font* was provided in the nave for baptisms. In the seventeenth century, especially during the time of Archbishop Laud, *communion rails* were provided round altars. *Seating*, already universal in parish churches, became gradually more common in cathedrals too.

Many screens were removed between about 1780 and 1840 when vistas were all the rage. Results of this process were disappointing: cathedrals now looked bare and empty and lost all sense of mystery. So the Victorians either put them back, or, if they had been destroyed, designed new ones.

Modern furnishings generally follow along the old lines, and the most recent reflect the revival of craftsmanship that has taken place since about 1960.

Lichfield — 'The Sleeping Children' by Chantrey

olour and decoration in cathedrals

Medieval decoration

Most medieval colour decoration in churches was educational in intent – illustrating the joys of Heaven and pains of Hell for the benefit of largely illiterate congregations. But this was not its sole purpose; it was just as popular and just as evident in the great monasteries and cathedrals, for art was itself an aspect of worship. Unfortunately, a great deal of its inspiration sprang from features which were eventually deemed idolatrous; thus, an injunction of Edward VI in 1547 read: '. . . take away, utterly extinct and destroy all shrines, coverings of shrines, all tables, candlesticks, trindles or rolls of wax, figures, paintings, and all other monuments of feigned miracles, pilgrimages, idolatry, and superstition. . . .'

Sometimes chapters managed to save their buildings from the worst excesses of iconoclasm: Canterbury and York, for example, saved most of their glass; mural paintings have sometimes painstakingly been recovered from under layers of whitewash; inaccessible statues sometimes survived intact; and other objects made their way into private collections. It therefore still remains possible to piece together some idea of what these great buildings really looked like in their prime.

Books

Books of all kinds were often richly illuminated with miniatures and other decorations. In the Dark Ages, Ireland led Western Europe in the field of manuscript art, and the Irish mission, first to Scotland, thence to Northumbria, spread the use of Irish techniques. Most manuscripts of this period are now in public collections, but the Gospels of St Chad are still in the cathedral library at Lichfield.

During late Saxon and early post-Conquest times there was a good deal of similarity between styles of illumination in Britain and in neighbouring parts of the Continent, especially France and Flanders. The great treasure of this period still in cathedral hands is the Winchester Bible of about 1150 to 1170.

Before the introduction of printing, book production was a time-consuming and expensive business. The preparation of the parchment or vellum included soaking, stretching, rubbing smooth with pumice, cutting to size, and ruling. Scribes made their own ink from hawthorn bark, lampblack, or charcoal, and cut their own goose quills. Illuminations, in water colour, were embellished with gold leaf, carefully glued in place and then polished with a pebble. Covers were made in various ways, but for fine books often had metalwork and enamelling, or even ivory and gemstones.

Painting

It was standard eleventh-century practice to plaster and paint exterior as well as interior walls. Much of the painting consisted simply of a pattern of ashlar stonework ruled on to whitewashed plaster – although, internally, large areas of wall would often have religious scenes painted on them instead; these murals were usually painted in distemper on a thin layer of fine plaster.

Colours were made from vegetable dyes, metal ores, and natural earths. Red predominated for it could be made cheaply from madder as well as from mercury ore. The best blue was the most expensive (made from *lapis lazuli*).

Eleventh-century mock-ashlar painting can be seen at St Albans. Good examples of twelfth-century murals can be seen in St Anselm's and St Gabriel's Chapels in Canterbury Cathedral, and work of the thirteenth century can be seen at Winchester and St Albans again.

As masoncraft improved, ashlar masonry, within and without, was left bare. Outside, however, the sculptural friezes in such places as Wells, Exeter, and Lichfield, were painted and gilded. Inside, some murals were still done, but instead of painting reredoses straight on to walls we find carved ones of stone or wood instead – all, originally, brightly coloured. Wood was prepared by adding fine layers of gesso – powdered chalk bound with glue – rubbed smooth. (Norwich contains some superb examples of painted wooden retables.) Screens were similarly painted and gilded, as were roof bosses, images, and funerary monuments – which, so far from being sombre, were a riot of harmonious colour.

From the late thirteenth century, painting on wood was usually done in tempera, that is, colour mixed with a white of egg base, or oils; that on stone or plaster was still done in distemper. Gilding was always done with gold leaf.

St Albans Cathedral: a medieval wall-painting of William Fitzherbert, Archbishop of York

Glass

Coloured glass, transmuting rather than reflecting light, was probably the most effective of all colour decoration in medieval buildings. Twelfth-century glass was made of pot-metal, that is, glass to which various metal oxides have been added before melting, and which is therefore coloured right through. It has characteristically rich, deep, glowing colours with reds and blues predominating. Nothing in later glass can surpass the twelfth-century windows in Canterbury and York.

But this early work, in small windows, made churches very dark, and, as windows grew larger, so glass grew lighter, and flash glass was more commonly used. This was made by coating white glass with a thin layer of coloured glass, giving a more transparent colour. Another light, and cheap, form was grisaille, which means grey-coloured. It contained mostly leaf and geometrical patterns, sometimes with medallions of coloured figure glass inserted. It was introduced in the thirteenth century, and can be seen at York and Salisbury.

In the fourteenth century, yellows and greens play a bigger part. Figures lost their sunburnt appearance when white glass replaced the pinky-brown previously used for flesh. Silver sulphide or chloride was introduced to produce yellows and oranges. This could be painted on before firing, and yellow and white could now be produced on the same piece of glass, which facilitated the making of haloed faces. Lombardic script, similar to our capitals, gave way to the black-letter script used in books, about 1375.

The fifteenth century concentrated on windows containing whole scenes, or groups of scenes, and, as an alternative, serried rows of figures.

Tiles

Floors were usually tiled, and the tiles generally carried stencilled patterns, often set together to form larger patterns. An expensive alternative occasionally favoured was *opus alexandrinum*, mosaic work in coloured marble: the floor of the Trinity Chapel at Canterbury was made in this style about 1220.

Textiles

By their nature perishable, few medieval textiles have survived. Embroidery reached its height in the thirteenth and early fourteenth centuries when English work, *opus anglicanum*, was considered the finest in Europe.

Although remaining pieces are mostly in museums, a few magnificent copes are still in use. These were usually made of velvet, silk, or satin, and then embroidered, often with gold and silver thread. The stitches were simple, but carefully adapted to the design. Before the Reformation, Lincoln Cathedral alone had more than 600 vestments decorated with embroidery, jewellery, and gold wire. That is the measure of what has been lost.

The most famous of all English medieval textiles still exists however, but in a French cathedral – the Bayeux tapestry, made in the late eleventh century.

Post-medieval decoration

The only new addition of colour in early post-Reformation times took the form of funerary monuments. Here the medieval tradition survived, though foreign marbles and Renaissance detail were used.

The true revival of colour decoration came as late as Bentley's Westminster, where it is used opulently, but there is no equivalent in Britain to the great baroque and rococo decorative schemes sometimes found in continental cathedrals.

Most eighteenth-century fitments in British cathedrals were removed by Victorian restorers – with the exception of monuments, which, though often of excellent quality, were nearly all made in black and white marbles which do little to enliven the buildings.

Glass

Most cathedral glass, except in Canterbury and York, is nineteenth century. Some of it is dingy, much is insipid, and even more is worthy but dull. A little, however, is very good, and among the best are Hedgeland's strangely Georgian-looking west window at Norwich, the west window of Worcester, and the Powells' work at Norwich Roman Catholic Cathedral.

Really new ground, however, was first broken by Burne-Jones, whose east window of the Latin Chapel in Oxford Cathedral (made by Powell in 1859) is marvellously alive in composition and rich in colour. Later Burne-Jones glass, both at Oxford, and at Birmingham and elsewhere, was less adventurous, and the brilliant promise in the Latin Chapel window was never quite fulfilled.

Indeed, it was not until the 1960s that exciting glass appeared again. Some of the best in the years between – like Douglas Strachan's windows at Glasgow and Dunblane – pleases greatly, but for real inspiration we had to wait for Coventry and the baptistery window (designed by John Piper and made by Patrick Reyntiens in 1962). Liverpool Metropolitan Cathedral, completed in 1967, has glass which is perhaps even more dramatic – such as that, again by Piper, in the corona. In the Blessed Sacrament Chapel in the same cathedral, Ceri Richards' glass – part of a complete decorative scheme, and as equally abstract as Piper's – uses simpler patterns and cooler colours. Henry Haig's work at Clifton, 1973, is also abstract, but the shapes are rounded and bubble-like – more fluid and dynamic than Piper's angularity, though less majestic and more restrained in colour.

Ensembles

Most Victorian ensembles have now been broken up, and a great deal of the furniture put into cathedrals during nineteenth-century restorations has been ejected as ruthlessly as the restorers themselves ejected anything in the classical taste. The trouble is that the accident of unfashionableness so often leads to an inability to distinguish between the good, the bad, and the indifferent. Scott's lush and opulent choirs of Worcester and Lichfield have become valuable, and, one hopes, increasingly valued survivals. Restored to their pristine state they are

A detail from one of the glass panels of Coventry Cathedral

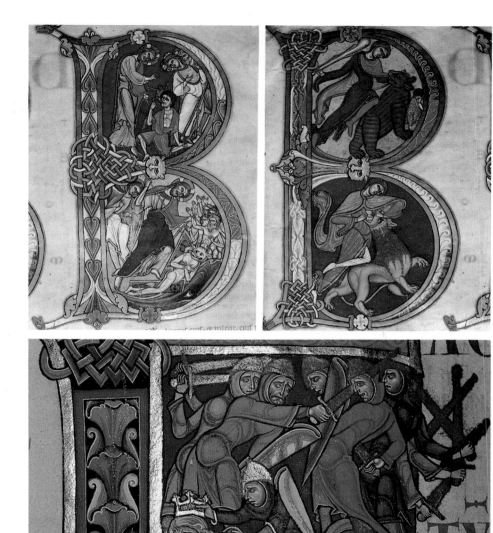

*Winchester: Three illuminated letters from the
Winchester Bible, c1150–70.*

Canterbury: Thomas Becket window, c1200.

20

*Birmingham: Ascension Window, by Sir Edward
Burne-Jones and William Morris, 1884.*

21

York Minster: Great East Window–detail: Murder of Abel, by John Thornton, 1405-08.

Salisbury: Tomb of Sir Richard Mompesson and his wife
Dame Catherine, 1627.

Coventry: Baptistery window, c1960, by John Piper and
Patrick Reyntiens.

24

Coventry: Copes: Ferial Green, Festival Yellow, and Advent Blue.

25

Lincoln: Dean's Eye–detail, early thirteenth century.

26

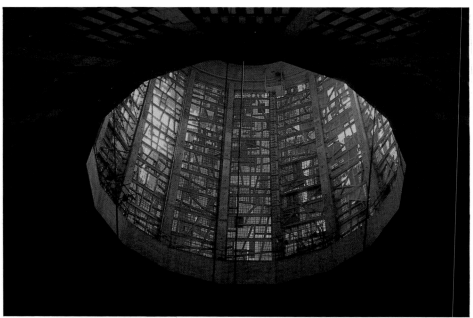

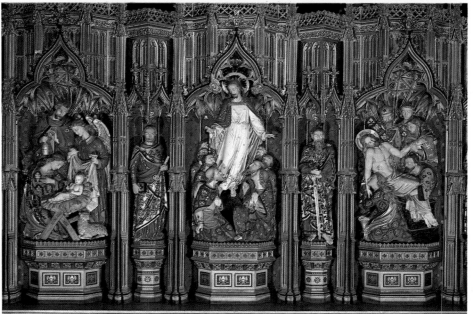

Top: Metropolitan Cathedral of Christ the King,
Liverpool: Lantern: glass by John Piper and
Patrick Reyntiens, c1965.

Bottom: Gloucester: The reredos of the High Altar, by
Sir G G Scott, 1873.

Chichester: Painting in St Mary Magdalene Chapel:
Noli me tangere, by Graham Sutherland, 1961.

Canterbury: St Paul: mural painting in St Anselm's
Chapel. Late twelfth century.

*Top: Westminster: The Symbol of Immortality: Mosaic,
by Boris Anrep, c1960.*

*Bottom: Bristol: Eastern Lady Chapel: altar, and tomb of
Abbot Newbury, 1473; tomb surround, c1300.*

Top: Chichester: Painting in the south transept:
Henry VIII and Bishop Sherburne, by Lambert Bernard,
c1520.

Bottom: Norwich: Painted retable in St Luke's Chapel,
c1380.

31

Canterbury: Mosaic pavement behind the High Altar:
Opus Alexandrinum, c1220.

Bristol

The Augustinian Abbey at Bristol was founded in 1140 by Robert Fitzharding, later Lord Berkeley. In 1542, shortly after the monastery had been dissolved, Henry VIII raised the church to cathedral rank. It ceased to be a bishop's seat in 1836, but the diocese was recreated in 1897.

Seen from the north across College Green, it is a fine sight, but not a particularly remarkable one, and visitors may enter the cathedral not expecting to see anything of much consequence. If so, they are in for a surprise, for the medieval work at Bristol, though its scale may be small, is among the most exciting in the country: the work of a brilliantly original, but now unknown architect.

The nave was built by G E Street between 1868 and 1888. His style is in general that of the late thirteenth century, which is a little earlier than the majority of the medieval work. Street, in fact, had three options open to him: he could have imitated the east end, creating a consistent building, but adding nothing to its interest; he could have ignored it, and gone his own way, but he was not a self-assertive man; or he could make his west front and nave lead up to the medieval work, and this could be done by adopting its general plan but omitting its eccentricities. This he did, and if the nave is not very memorable, that is probably what he intended: it is in harmony with the medieval work, but it makes no attempt to rival it.

Entry is by the north porch, and Street does alert us at once to one of the most original aspects of Bristol. It is a hall-church; that is, the central vessel and the side aisles are of equal height, and there is therefore no triforium or clerestory. Bristol is, indeed, one of the earliest large-scale hall-churches in existence, and may have been one of the sources of the extensive development of this form in late medieval Germany.

Off the north chancel aisle is the Elder Lady Chapel. This is earlier than the rest of the cathedral, completed about 1220, and largely dependent on Wells. The new chancel was begun in 1298 and completed about 1330. Although only 50ft high, an impression of greater height is obtained by the way in which the mouldings of the piers go straight up into the arches, interrupted by capitals only on the small shafts on the north and south sides – an innovation which subsequently became very popular.

Another innovation lies in the vault, for it is the earliest high lierne vault in existence.

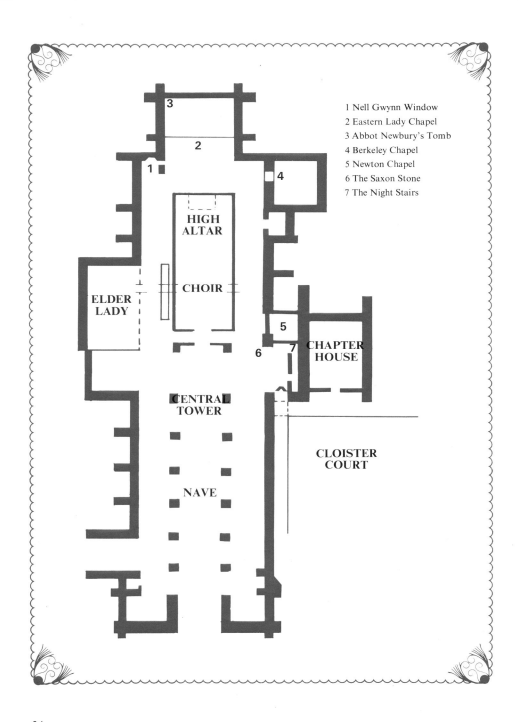

1 Nell Gwynn Window
2 Eastern Lady Chapel
3 Abbot Newbury's Tomb
4 Berkeley Chapel
5 Newton Chapel
6 The Saxon Stone
7 The Night Stairs

3

2

1

4

HIGH
ALTAR

CHOIR

ELDER
LADY

5

6 **7** CHAPTER
HOUSE

CENTRAL
TOWER

CLOISTER
COURT

NAVE

Liernes were not invented here, but probably in London, where they occur in the undercroft of St Stephen's Chapel, Westminster, but this is their first large scale use. They are, indeed, emphasized, first by the omission of the ridge-rib, and secondly by the way in which they, and they alone of the vaulting ribs, are ornamented by cusps. This design was taken up and developed a few years later at Wells and elsewhere.

The hall-church plan makes normal flying buttresses impossible, and the problem arose of how to carry the thrust of the chancel vault to the aisle walls. It was solved by yet another innovation: the flying buttresses are taken across the aisles like stone tiebeams, arch-braced beneath; that is, the design is based on timber roofs in parish churches. But the aisles are vaulted, and the tiebeams cross the aisles like bridges at the point where the vault springs from the walls. So instead of vaulting the aisles in one sweep, the designer brought them down steeply in the middle to touch the flying buttresses, making a delicate stalactite effect.

The window tracery of the chancel aisles is as inventive as one would expect from this master, moving well away from geometrical designs towards the flowing patterns shortly to come into fashion. The east window of the north chancel aisle contains late seventeenth-century glass said to have been given by Nell Gwynne.

The chancel reredos was put in by Pearson in 1899 and blends well with the medieval work. The stalls date from about 1520, with flamboyant, that is French-style, tracery, and good misericords.

East of the chancel lies the Eastern Lady Chapel. This is part of the same building operation as the chancel, and is also designed as a hall-church. Its big east window is remarkable in its tracery for c 1300. The reredos and sedilia are part of the original design, and have been recoloured by Tristram on the basis of remaining fragments. So have the tomb recesses.

From the south chancel aisle one reaches the Berkeley Chapel, known to have been in use by 1309. The vestibule leading to it has an extraordinary vault, even by Bristol standards. It is actually a flat stone ceiling with ribs forming a sort of Union Jack pattern, but there are also ribs springing from the wall in normal fashion to make a quadripartite rib vault. However, they are just a skeleton: the cells are left empty so that the flat ceiling can be seen behind, forming yet another experiment with voids and vistas of which this architect was so fond. Big bosses at the junctions tie the composition firmly together.

The Berkeley Chapel itself is less experimental, and has fairly standard vaulting and fenestration. The fine and rare fifteenth-century brass candelabra came from the nearby Temple Church.

The Newton Chapel, further west, was added a little later: a simpler affair altogether. It contains some nice monuments, including a baroque one to Sir John Newton, 1661, and a beauty by Westmacott to Elizabeth Stanhope, 1816.

The cathedral's transepts and crossing are basically Norman, extensively remodelled about 1500. The vaults are interesting as a much later interpretation of the theme of the chancel. The screen is by Pearson, and the pulpit incorporates flamboyant fragments from its early sixteenth-century predecessor, carved in the same spirit as the choir stalls. In the south transept is a very interesting carving of the harrowing of hell, certainly older than the monastery, and probably dating from about 1050. Here, too, can be seen the worn Night Stairs leading from the Canons' dormitory.

It is worth going now to the cloister, the east range of which contains the chapter house. This is a spirited piece of late Norman work of the third quarter of the twelfth century. It is rib-vaulted with intersecting blank arcading above the stalls. Alternate shafts are spiral-banded and there is a variety of capitals. Above this again is a vigorous scheme of decoration of trellis work leading up to a vast array of zig-zag. Zig-zag is also very much in evidence in the vaulting ribs. A new refectory was built at the south east corner in 1968.

Canterbury

Canterbury, founded by St Augustine in 597, is not only the senior cathedral in England, but also the mother church of the world-wide Anglican communion.

Nothing is left of the Saxon cathedral, and remarkably little of the one built by Lanfranc, the first Norman archbishop. Rather more is left of the additions made by Prior Ernulf at the beginning of the twelfth century, and financed in part by Archbishop Anselm, but most of what we see belongs either to the few years after 1174 at the east end, or to the end of the fourteenth century when the nave was rebuilt. A few features are later still, including the principal towers.

The close is entered through Christ Church Gate in the south-west corner. From here the cathedral, though built of Caen stone, gives the misleading impression of being the epitome of English medieval architecture,

with its twin western towers, a tall tower over the crossing, and its great length (547ft).

Bell Harry, the 249ft crossing tower, dominates the cathedral. It was built by John Wastell about 1500, with octagonal corner turrets which terminate in openwork lanterns totally different in effect from those at Gloucester. The most interesting feature of this beautifully proportioned tower is that it is built of brick, and only faced with stone.

The western towers look a perfect pair. In fact the northern one was completed in 1841, a copy by Austin of the southern one built by Thomas Mapilton about 1430. The balance thus achieved cost the destruction of Lanfranc's north-west tower, finished about 1080. Its appearance is known from drawings, and it seems that the modest height of Mapilton's tower was due to his desire to match the earlier one.

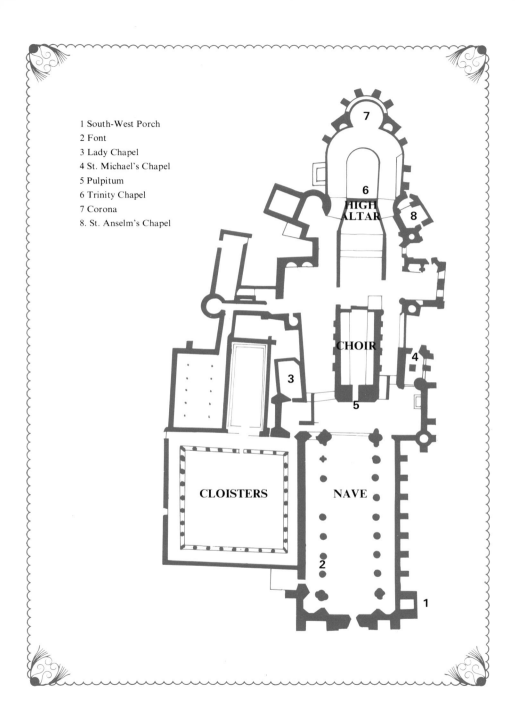

1 South-West Porch
2 Font
3 Lady Chapel
4 St. Michael's Chapel
5 Pulpitum
6 Trinity Chapel
7 Corona
8. St. Anselm's Chapel

7

6

HIGH
ALTAR

8

CHOIR

4

3

5

CLOISTERS

NAVE

2

1

The other towers are really no more than turrets. They stand in the re-entrant angles of the east transepts, and belong to the rebuilding of the chancel between 1096 and 1130. The southern one, known as Anselm's tower, was heightened later in the twelfth century, and carries a small lead-clad cap.

The exterior of the eastern half of the church is an attractive muddle, and it is better to first go inside where the features are easier to understand. One enters by the south-west porch into Henry Yeveley's serenely beautiful nave, built between 1391 and 1405, one of the finest creations of English Gothic. Like Wynford's nave at Winchester, it is a remodelling of early Norman work. Yeveley recased the piers in an up-to-date form, and raised the roof level to that of the chancel. Since the chancel stands on a tall crypt, this means the nave is high by English standards, 80ft from floor to vault. The triforium and clerestory form a single composition, though a transom preserves their separate identities. Tall aisles allow large windows, and the interior is very light. Both nave and aisles carry lierne vaults.

The font is a restrained classical composition, in black and white marble, of 1639. The great canopy of a former archbishop's throne was carved by Grinling Gibbons in 1704. The west window contains some reset twelfth-century glass. The early glass of Canterbury, probably dating from just before 1200, is among the best of any period in England, though there is little doubt that it was made by French craftsmen. A great deal of it has been moved from its original setting, but although this makes nonsense of the iconographical schemes, and spoils the ensemble at the east end, it does not sully one's enjoyment of its beauty, with its fine figure drawing and superbly rich colour.

The best monument in the nave is that to Orlando Gibbons, the composer; the most unusual, that to the Hales family, includes a representation of Sir James Hales' suicide, and the younger Sir James' burial at sea.

The transepts at the crossing are partly Norman in their walling, but fifteenth century in all essentials, especially the great north and south windows. The north window still has some of the glass donated by Edward IV in 1482. It was in this transept that Becket was murdered in 1170. The monuments include a fine one to Archbishop Peckham, 1292, and a sumptuous one to Archbishop Warham, 1532, Cranmer's predecessor, and thus the last pre-Reformation holder of the office. To the east of this transept is the fan-vaulted Lady Chapel.

The crossing tower also has a fan-vault, very high up, for Bell Harry is emphatically a lantern. In the south transept south window are three rows of twelfth-century glass figures moved from further east. To the east of this transept is a two-storeyed annexe with St Michael's Chapel on the ground floor, lierne-vaulted, and containing many recoloured monuments from the fifteenth century onwards. Above is All Saints' Chapel, accessible from the south chancel aisle. It has a simpler tierceron vault.

At the crossing, instead of going up into the choir, it is best first to go down into the crypt – more of a ground floor church than simply an underground chamber. It was built for Anselm's choir about 1096. The piers correspond to the chancel piers above – two of them added in 1176 as part of the rebuilding. Its 'nave' is further subdivided into three by rows of columns. These are fascinating. Some of them have fluted designs, and most have superbly carved capitals, full of life and vigour.

Chapel of Our Lady of the Undercroft

Effigy of the Black Prince

The south transept of the crypt was remodelled as the Black Prince's chantry in 1363, and is lierne-vaulted as against the groined vaults of the crypt as a whole. The east part of the nave forms the Chapel of Our Lady of the Undercroft, with beautiful late fourteenth-century stone screens.

The quality of the best early Saxon carving can be gauged from the eight fragments of the cross and the columns of the chancel screen brought here from Reculver. Both probably belong to the period immediately after the foundation of the abbey there in 669.

The apse of St Gabriel's Chapel was walled up in the late twelfth century, and when the wall was reopened in the nineteenth century, its wall paintings, dating from about 1130, were found to be excellently preserved, and of first class quality. The inspiration is clearly Byzantine.

Further east is the Trinity Chapel crypt, taller than the earlier work – as the Trinity Chapel is raised above even the level of the choir – and dating from about 1178. This is Gothic work : the vaults are ribbed and the arches are pointed, but the change will be more readily understood when we look at the work above. Purbeck marble is used, and there is a characteristic change in emphasis from carvings to mouldings. This was not because Purbeck will not carve well : numerous monuments prove that it will. It was simply due to a greater appreciation of the texture of materials in architectural composition; no longer were all the bones designed to be hidden under plaster or whitewash. The large Caen stone boss of acanthus leaves at the far east end, under the Corona, is all the more effective for standing virtually alone.

Returning to main floor level, one climbs more steps to enter the choir through Prior Chillenden's pulpitum – put in about 1400. The figures of kings in the niches are original, and good for their date, as are the iron gates.

The furniture in the choir is pleasant but not especially distinguished. What is of note is the architecture. There were three main sources of English Gothic, all of which seem to have sprung up in the 1170s. One is the Cistercian inspired work in the north, to be seen, for example, at Ripon. Another is the beautiful indigenous development at Wells, with its far-reaching effect upon the churches of the west. The third is the east end of Canterbury.

The Canterbury work was the happy outcome of two disasters: Becket was murdered in 1170, and in 1174, Anselm's chancel was gutted by fire. The immediate popularity of Becket's tomb meant both that rapid reconstruction was doubly important and that ample funds were available for the purpose. In curiously modern fashion the design was opened to international competition. The architect chosen was William of Sens, who had worked at Sens Cathedral and perhaps elsewhere in the early Gothic idiom of the Ile de France. This he proceeded to use at Canterbury, with the result that, in spite of Yeveley's nave, Canterbury is the least English of English cathedrals. For William it was both triumph and tragedy: triumph in the success of his design despite the difficulty of adapting it to the strange lines of the existing outer walls and crypt; tragedy in being crippled by a fall from the scaffolding and having to return to France before the completion of his work – which was finished in a similar, but not identical style, by William the Englishman.

In nearly every case William of Sens'

piers rose where the previous ones had stood, and the odd shape of the presbytery, which canted inwards, and then outwards again to form the Trinity Chapel, was an inherited peculiarity. Round and octagonal piers are used alternately, not for the first time in England, but undoubtedly the inspiration for what soon became a popular fashion. The capitals, with their acanthus leaves, are typically French, and so is the sexpartite vault. In the curve of the apse the pillars are so close together that the arches are stilted to match the height of those to north and south. Purbeck marble is used, sparingly, for shafts and abaci. Were it not for the screens of the monuments set between the piers, this work would still convey the cool simplicity of the original design. Gothic was to produce finer work than this, nowhere more obviously than in Yeveley's nave, but, as at Wells, one feels strongly that the potential is all there. It is a powerful piece of building.

The north chancel aisle has dogtooth in its vault ribs, perhaps where this very popular ornament was first used. The windows are Prior Ernulf's, big for their date, and two of them containing late twelfth-century glass with New Testament scenes flanked by the Old Testament events that foreshadowed them. These, and all the other early windows at an accessible height, deserve every minute of attention that one can afford to give them, for they are among the great art treasures of medieval Britain. Three archbishops lie here in splendour: Chichele, 1443, Bourchier, 1486, and Howley, 1848. Bourchier's monument is made of Bethersden marble, a Kentish equivalent of Purbeck.

The east transepts are, exceptionally, longer than those at the main crossing. They both have two small apsed chapels on the east side. The northern one has twelfth-century glass in the rose window.

Next, St Andrew's Chapel. This, like St Anselm's, its equivalent on the south side, is canted strongly inwards towards the Trinity Chapel. The alignment of piers and walls in this part of the building almost forms a segment of a circle.

Eight of the Trinity Chapel ambulatory

windows still have their original glass. These show the miracles of St Thomas, whose shrine lay within the chapel. The glass is unlikely to be later than about 1200, and could be as early as 1180. The number of miracles that could be shown so soon after the Saint's death is a vivid indication of the rate of growth of his cult. Templates seem to have been used to design the figures, for some are identical in posture, while others have the same outline in reverse. The Purbeck monument here is Archbishop Walter's, 1205. In the Trinity Chapel itself lie the Black Prince, 1376, with his effigy in copper gilt, Henry IV, 1413, and his Queen, Joan of Navarre, 1437, in alabaster, and Dean Wotton, 1567. All of them are ambitious, exhibiting technical virtuosity rather than great artistry – though Henry IV's effigy seems close to portraiture, an uncommon refinement in the Middle Ages, even if not unknown on royal tombs. The pavement of this chapel, laid down about 1220 to stand before Becket's shrine, is one of the best in England.

The piers here are coupled, a design used at Sens, though this is William the Englishman's work. Presumably he was keeping to the existing plan. The differences between the work of the French and the English William may be seen in the details of the gallery and clerestory, and it is interesting to note the visible alterations which demonstrate that it was the Englishman's idea to raise the floor of the Trinity Chapel above the level of the choir.

At the extreme east end is the Corona, a near circular chapel connected originally with the cultus of Becket. It is a small room of great charm, with its original glass, and the thirteenth-century chair, known as St Augustine's, used at the enthronement of new archbishops.

For a change, it is not the glass that catches the eye in St Anselm's Chapel, but wall painting – featuring a magnificent mid twelfth-century St Paul shaking off the viper. When one looks at the paintings in this and St Gabriel's Chapel, and at the glass here at Canterbury, one begins to visualise the overwhelming magnificence that such a cathedral possessed in its prime. The monument to Archbishop Meopham, 1333, forms a screen across the opening to the chapel. It has its original iron gates, delightful small sculpture, and split-cusped ('Kentish') tracery.

The south-east transept has the last of the twelfth-century glass, which can be contrasted with the work of Erwin Bossanyi, 1960. The doe-eyed faces in Bossanyi's work are attractive, but one misses the dignity natural to the early figures. This glass will doubtless be better appreciated as time goes on. Now, the inevitable comparison with near-contemporary work by people like Piper, Richards, and New is unfair to it, for it stands at the end of the previous tradition, and is greatly superior to most earlier twentieth-century work.

The south chancel aisle contains thirteenth-century French glass, which can also be compared with the earlier glass further east, and three fine monuments. Prior Eastry, 1322, and Archbishop Stratford, 1348, have particularly good effigies, Stratford's being an early example of the use of alabaster; Archbishop Kempe's, 1454, has a splendid wooden spired canopy, reminiscent in some ways of the best fourteenth-century work.

The precincts at Canterbury lie to the north. In the time of Lanfranc, Christ Church was the largest monastery in England – with nearly 150 monks – and the ruins of the vast dormitory completed in his time are impressive. The lierne-vaulted cloister was rebuilt about 1400. The chapter house, off the east walk, is rectangular, and 90ft long. It was built by Prior Eastry in 1304, but the windows were altered later by Chillenden.

The infirmary hall and chapel, in eloquent ruin, form a single composition, 250ft long, and as early as c 1100.

There is far more to see than can possibly be mentioned here, but perhaps enough has been noted to make it obvious that one cannot hurry over Canterbury. Some cathedrals, even highly interesting ones, can be seen fairly adequately in an hour if time is short. Even a cursory examination of Canterbury will take nearer two.

oventry

The Benedictine monastery at Coventry was founded by Leofric and Godiva in 1043. At the beginning of the twelfth century it became a cathedral, and the diocese was known as Coventry and Lichfield. When the priory was dissolved the cathedral became redundant and was dismantled, the only one in England to disappear as a result of the Reformation. The modern diocese was founded in 1918, and the great parish church of St Michael became the bishop's seat. It was gutted by bombs in 1940, and remains as a glorious ruin, forming a forecourt to the new cathedral designed by Sir Basil Spence in 1951.

The new cathedral was completed in 1962. It lies at right angles to the old cathedral, and is built of the same local pink sandstone.

Spence had to satisfy his clients and at the same time produce a building in which he himself could believe. Anglican cathedrals since St Paul's had all been designed in the Gothic style, and for many the Gothic conception of a cathedral was still the only valid one. There were also those, of course, who would have preferred something more radical along the lines of the slightly later Catholic cathedral at Liverpool. The success of Spence's building lies in the fact that it is not a compromise, but a transition, a genuine, and major, step forward, as architecturally valid as, say, St Hugh's choir at Lincoln, and undeniably beautiful.

For Coventry is a design of subtlety and imagination which puts it into a different class from the scholarly conservatism of, say, Truro or St Edmundsbury, Liverpool (Anglican) or Guildford. And, unlike those less fortunate cathedrals, Spence could call on

the finest artists and craftsmen of the day to produce the furnishings. (It was in this respect far truer to medieval precedent than any of the churches of the Gothic revival, none of which is rich in fittings.)

Luckily the west steeple of the old church survived the bombs, for at 295ft high it is only rivalled among parish churches by Louth, and exceeded among cathedrals by Salisbury, Norwich, and Liverpool (Anglican). The tower was completed by 1394, and the spire by 1433. The transition from tower to spire is made by means of an octagonal drum connected to the pinnacles by flying buttresses.

At the east end of the old cathedral is a polygonal apse, a rare feature in England, doubtless inspired in this instance by the Lady Chapel at Lichfield. The ruins have become a symbol of reconciliation. The crosses are made of nails and charred beams salvaged from the ruins, as were the stones of the high altar, set up by the cathedral stonemason only two months after the bombing. On the wall behind it are carved the words 'Father forgive'. In the crypt is the former Chapel of Unity, the witness of many post-war ecumenical activities before the new one was completed.

From the outside the new cathedral is unpretentious but promising. On the east side (ritual south), the gently swelling curve with its huge window marks the baptistery, and the chapter-house-like projection at the north-east corner is the Guild Chapel. On the west, the big projection at the south end is the new Chapel of Unity. On both sides, the concertina shape of the walls enables light to be thrown from the south on to the high altar. The flèche makes no attempt to rival the medieval steeple. The porch, on a huge scale, and open on three sides, makes a brilliant transition from the old church to the new.

To its east, near the baptistery window, is Epstein's *St Michael and Lucifer*, treated with an unexpected conservatism compared to his earlier work. There is little dynamism in the forms, and the most telling feature is the compassion on the face of St Michael as he stands victorious over his enemy.

The vast wall of clear glass engraved by John Hutton was the first major use of this method of decoration in any British cathedral. The figures are more stylized and up-to-date than Epstein's, but more medieval in the way in which form and gesture rather than expression speak their intent.

Inside, one is in a Gothic building. This may not strike home at once, for it is a restatement so imaginative that there is nothing whatsoever of reproduction about it. But it is Gothic in its longitudinal plan; Gothic in its form of nave and aisles separated by piers; Gothic in its ceiling canopy which deliberately recalls vaulting; and Gothic in the canopied form of its choir stalls. At the same time it is uncompromisingly twentieth century: from the (ritual) west end one sees no side windows, just bare walls with texts carved on them; the piers are of a slimness undreamed of even by the master

Epstine's powerful sculpture of
St Michael and Lucifer

who built the Salisbury Lady Chapel; and a great tapestry dominates the presbytery, not a great window (which would hardly have been suitable anyway as the cathedral faces north).

The baptistery is bathed in light from the huge curved window filled with abstract glass by John Piper, with darker colours near the edges, but forming a great pool of gold at the centre. The font is an enormous uncarved sandstone boulder from near Bethlehem. The biblical inscriptions on the walls were designed and handcut by Ralph Beyer.

The first of the side windows one sees are much more restless in composition than Piper's baptistery window, but as one walks towards the altar, a greater tranquility develops. Sir Basil Spence explained this as a parable of life, in that the colour of the windows is only revealed as you reach each stage: the past is known whereas the future is not. The whole range of colour can only be seen when one has reached the altar.

The windows were designed by Lawrence Lee, Geoffrey Clarke, and Keith New, and the colours chosen were green and yellow to represent youth, pink and red for adolescence and passion, multi-coloured for the age of experience, deep blue and purple for wisdom, and finally, gold.

The Chapel of Unity has a splendid mosaic floor by Einar Forseth, and glowing abstract glass by Margaret Traherne. This chapel is the answer to those who object that modern cathedrals have nothing of the sense of mystery to be found in their medieval predecessors: here is a numinosity as intense as any to be found in York, a clear proof that such atmosphere can be architecturally contrived, and does not have to be the product of centuries of aging and mellowing. The ground plan is a star, in remembrance of Christ's birth; the elevation is in the shape of a crusader's tent, to represent the crusade for unity; and at the centre of the mosaic floor is a dove, symbol of the Holy Spirit.

Going now to the choir: the pulpit, lectern, and stalls were all designed by Spence, as was the arrangement of the organ pipes. The canopies of the stalls are simple in design, but rich in symbolism. The bronze eagle of the lectern was the work of Elizabeth Frink. The altar cross was by Geoffrey Clarke, conveying abstractly the agony of the cross rather as one sees it representationally in late medieval paintings.

Graham Sutherland's tapestry of *Christ in Glory* was woven in France by Pinton Frères. More controversy has surrounded this than any other item in the cathedral. It is immense, and, at $75\frac{1}{2}$ft, a little higher than the vault of Durham. The tiny human figure is, incredibly, life size. Thus Christ is compared to man. As the cathedral can be said to be an entirely fresh interpretation of Gothic, using different idioms and constructional techniques, so the tapestry can be said to be an equally free interpretation of Byzantine mosaics and paintings in a different medium. The seated figure of Christ, in a vesica-shaped surround, is flanked by symbols of the evangelists with flashes of a fiery red above them. From on high stream the rays of heaven. Below is a chalice and an agonized crucifixion forming a reredos for the Lady Chapel altar.

The Guild Chapel's chief ornament is a crown of thorns by Geoffrey Clarke. The Chapel of Gethsemane has a crown of thorns screen designed by Spence, and a byzantinesque angel and sleeping disciples by Steven Sykes. It is always bathed in a golden light.

One cannot do better than sum up this cathedral by recalling the expressed intention of its architect not to solve a planning problem, but to create a shrine to the glory of God. That is how it, and indeed, all other cathedrals, should ultimately be appreciated.

Special Occasions
A new building generates new ideas, and Coventry was one of the first cathedrals to reappraise its role in the light of contemporary needs. Now, with its stage, it is better equipped than ever to fulfil it, and although there are no regular dates to be noted here, visitors will find a varied programme of events at almost any time of the year.

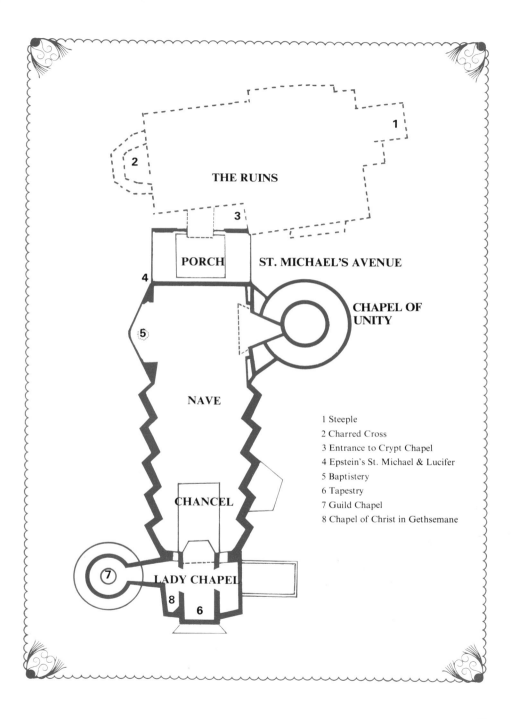

THE RUINS

PORCH

ST. MICHAEL'S AVENUE

CHAPEL OF
UNITY

NAVE

CHANCEL

LADY CHAPEL

1 Steeple
2 Charred Cross
3 Entrance to Crypt Chapel
4 Epstein's St. Michael & Lucifer
5 Baptistery
6 Tapestry
7 Guild Chapel
8 Chapel of Christ in Gethsemane

Dunblane

The ecclesiastical settlement at Dunblane dates from the early seventh century, but, although there were earlier bishops, the foundation of a territorial diocese took place about 1150. Much of the cathedral was built in the thirteenth century. It is small: nevertheless it is a building of great charm, and, though it dominates the small town in which it stands, it does so modestly. After the Reformation the chancel became a parish church, while the nave was allowed to fall into ruin. It was repaired and reroofed in 1893 by Sir Rowand Anderson, who also designed many of the fittings, and the chancel was restored by Sir Robert Lorimer in 1914.

The earliest part of the building is the lower part of the tower, dating from the beginning of the twelfth century. The nave, differently orientated, was built round it so that the tower now juts into it rather oddly, but it gives a much needed accent to the south elevation of a cathedral which has no transepts. It was heightened later, and the parapet was added later still, about 1500. It contains nine bells, designed by Lord Grimthorpe, who was mercifully not allowed to alter the structure of the cathedral as he did at St Albans.

The nave is confusing, for, although it seems to be of one build, the details span a considerable period. It may have been begun about 1240–50 and completed around 1300

or a little later. It is rather low, with only two storeys, there being no triforium or gallery, but the piers and arches are finely moulded. The aisle windows have groups of lancets, but by the time the clerestory had been reached, bar tracery had arrived, and the doubled tracery in the openings probably depend on the Angel Choir at Lincoln or the Chapel of the Nine Altars at Durham.

In the south-west buttress a small chapel (known as the Clement Chapel, after St Clement, Bishop of Dunblane 1233–58), was contrived in 1964 by Edith Burnet Hughes. It contains a *Christ in Majesty* by Maxwell Allan, a book of prayers by Helen Lamb, and glass by Gordon Webster. Returning to the nave, the baptistery window is by Douglas Strachan, 1926, and there is some interesting slightly earlier glass by Louis Davis.

At the west end stand six canopied stalls, dating from about 1490, a rare survival in Scotland, and standing next to them is a fine Pictish cross-slab, probably dating from the ninth or tenth century. The pulpit, like the screen and lectern, is the work of Sir Rowand Anderson. The iron light fittings were installed in 1935, handwrought, with a variety of symbolic panels.

The chancel, which has a single-storeyed elevation, is much the same age as the nave. The tall windows resulting from the absence of aisles are effective, and in some ways reminiscent of the Lichfield Lady Chapel. The stalls, organ case, and the screen behind the communion table were designed by Lorimer. Either side of the communion table are more stalls, without canopies, a little earlier than those at the west end, and with simple misericords. The south windows contain glass by Louis Davis.

The Lady Chapel stands to the north of the chancel. It was built about 1240, and is the only vaulted part of the cathedral. It contains glass by Douglas Strachan and Gordon Webster.

Externally the chancel windows are as impressive as they are inside, and the close rhythm of buttress and window makes a taut composition with little wall space, and consequently no need for ornament. The parapet was added about 1500.

The west front of the nave was highly praised by Ruskin, especially the foliage of the vesica window high in the gable: 'He was no common man who designed that Cathedral of Dunblane. I know not anything so perfect in its simplicity, and so beautiful, as far as it reaches, in all the Gothic with which I am acquainted.' The foliage, as Ruskin goes on to point out, is naturalistic, and again points to a date late in the thirteenth century. The west doorway, with its blank arcading, must once have been very fine, though now it is sadly worn and all the shafts are missing. It could easily date from about 1240.

Special Occasion

October – Festival of the Society of Friends of Dunblane Cathedral; a short service followed by a lecture and/or musical programme. Non-members may attend.

The West Door

Durham

It is a pity that so few visitors to Durham come by rail, for the view of the castle, cathedral, and monastery from the station must be among the half dozen or so finest architectural views in Europe. The cathedral stands on a loop of the Wear, guarded on the landward side by the castle, a reminder that the Bishops of Durham were expected to guard the Scottish border from late Saxon times onwards, and, from the thirteenth century till 1836, were officially styled Prince-Bishops.

The original site of the bishopric was Lindisfarne, where it was founded by St Aidan in 635. After the Danish raids it was wherever the monks responsible for the body of St Cuthbert happened to be. They settled at Chester-le-Street in 883, and finally at Durham in 995.

The present cathedral was begun in 1093 during the episcopate of William of St

Carileph, a fairly late start for a Norman rebuilding, and the year, for example, that Winchester was consecrated. Durham was not consecrated until 1133. However, the building of those forty years is both visually impressive and historically important. It incorporates rib-vaults, the earliest of any significance in Europe, pointed arches in connection with them, and, hidden in the gallery roof, flying buttresses to support them. Thus, the three classic elements of Gothic architecture are present already in this grandest and most monumental example of Norman Romanesque. Unfortunately the name of the designer is no longer known.

The best approach to the cathedral for those who do not mind a steepish walk is by way of the eighteenth-century Prebends' Bridge, from which the trees on the slopes above the river form a perfect foil to the mass of stonework rising above them. But from whatever direction one approaches, the harmonious relation of the three towers, though several centuries separate them, is the abiding impression.

The normal entrance is by the nave north

The Sanctuary Knocker on the north door

door—on which is fixed the famous twelfth century bronze sanctuary knocker, a superb piece of work, lacking now the enamelled eyes that once animated it, but retaining nevertheless a vivid sense of life and power.

The nave of Durham is one of the most exciting experiences in British architecture. Visitors from further south will feel at once how different it is from such Norman naves as Ely, Peterborough, Chichester, Gloucester, Rochester, or Norwich. It is worth asking one's self exactly what it is that is so different about Durham, and although part of the difference is intangible, spiritual perhaps, it is perfectly possible to analyse how the impression is created.

The first thing one notices is not really the most important, though it magnetizes the eyes. This is the incised decoration on the round piers. Columns in Romanesque churches were frequently painted; sculptural decoration, also probably coloured originally, is less common. However, the piers at Durham set a fashion followed as far away as Dunfermline Abbey, Fife, in one direction, and Waltham Abbey, Essex, in the other. More important, though, is the fact that the piers alternate much more strongly than in other surviving Norman buildings. The masts that customarily mark Norman bay divisions, at Durham rise only in alternate bays where the piers are compound. Durham is also rare in having an original Norman high vault, and this, too, is organized in double bays, with a pointed transverse arch at each compound pier. The combined effect of piers in vaulting is of a nave built up of square units, each of a double bay, what Byzantine architects called a tetrapylon. Thus although it is comparable in length with other Norman naves, and no wider, Durham does not have the same tunnel-like effect. The designer did not, of course, have to go to Byzantium for his prototype. A similar, though less mature arrangement was to be found in the Abbey of Jumièges in Normandy, and, apparently, in Edward the Confessor's Westminster Abbey.

Finally, the proportions of arcade, gallery and clerestory are different. There is neither the near-equality of storeys to be found at Ely or Norwich, nor the rigorous subordination of the upper storeys to the arcade to be found at Gloucester. Once again, indeed, Durham anticipates Gothic, and the proportions of the elevation are quite close to those of St Hugh's choir at Lincoln. The whole structure combines technical skill with a strong sense of composition. It was completed in 1133, and, apart from the introduction of zig-zag ornament, perhaps for the first time in England, carries through the original design begun in the chancel in 1093 without alteration.

The nave is admirably uncluttered, which not only enables its architecture to be enjoyed unimpeded, but also shows to advantage such excellent furnishings as there are. The font and its great wooden canopy date from 1663. The canopy skilfully mixes Gothic and Renaissance motifs. Twenty years later, the Father Smith organ case was made in quite a different spirit – as beautifully baroque a piece as one could wish to find in an English cathedral. The Miners' Memorial is an effective modern adaptation of English and

A 12th-century painting of St Cuthbert

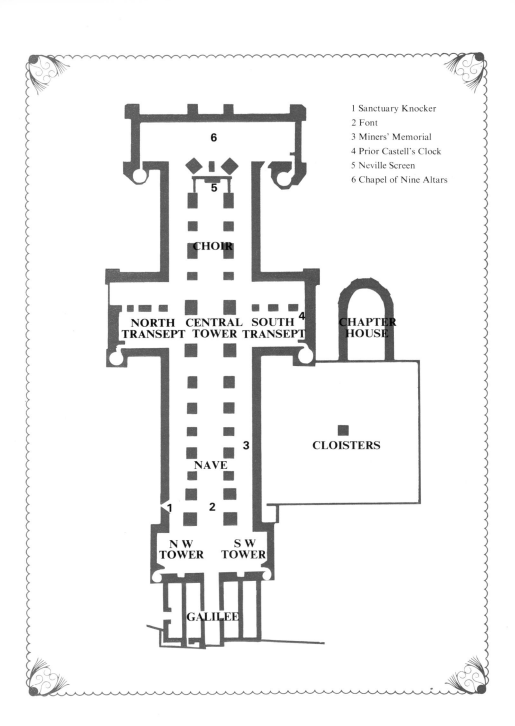

1 Sanctuary Knocker
2 Font
3 Miners' Memorial
4 Prior Castell's Clock
5 Neville Screen
6 Chapel of Nine Altars

6

5

CHOIR

NORTH   CENTRAL   SOUTH   4   CHAPTER
TRANSEPT   TOWER   TRANSEPT   HOUSE

3   CLOISTERS

NAVE

1   2

N W   S W
TOWER   TOWER

GALILEE

Spanish seventeenth-century fragments. Finally, there are two fine doors leading to the cloister on the south side: the prior's door with a wealth of Norman geometrical ornament, and the monks' door with its vigorous original ironwork still intact.

Going eastwards, the crossing and transepts are basically intact. Above the crossing, the details of the tower belong to the fifteenth century. The large windows in the transepts are also late medieval. The clock dates from about 1500, though it was substantially altered in 1630.

The chancel is the original work started in the time of Bishop William of St Carileph in 1093. It was complete, with the transepts, by 1104. The original high vault was replaced by the present one in the thirteenth century, but the aisle vaults are still as they were in 1104, and here one is looking at the direct ancestors of all the rib-vaults of whatever kind – not only in Britain, but in most of Western Europe.

The reredos, known as the Neville Screen, was completed in 1380, forming a single composition with the sedilia. Originally it held 107 alabaster statues, and with its delicate spired canopies it must have been extremely beautiful in its pristine state.

The stalls and the parclose screens behind them, like the font canopy, are of Bishop Cosin's time. Two zealous Protestant deans in the late sixteenth century, and Scottish prisoners in 1650 had smashed up most of the medieval woodwork, and Durham was fortunate in having a bishop at the Restoration whose enlightened patronage enabled the damage to be made good so effectively. In style only a little later, but in fact made in 1940, are the communion rails by Hollis.

The throne, given by Bishop Hatfield, who died in 1381, stands on top of his chantry chapel. This unique composition, restored in the seventeenth century, is said to give the Bishop of Durham the highest throne in christendom.

The need to provide more altar space resulted in the creation of the Chapel of Nine Altars – designed by Richard of Farnham

about 1235, though not completed in his lifetime. Many of the windows are lancets, deeply recessed to allow wall passages, and generously shafted, with alternate shafts in Frosterley marble.

The south window was inserted in the fifteenth century, but the north, or Joseph window, is original. Its great feeling of depth is created by doubling the main lines of the tracery on the inside. It was erected at the end of the work, about 1280, and was no part of Richard Farnham's design. Although it is clearly dependent on the east window of the Angel Choir at Lincoln, completed a few years earlier, it is a less classical, more varied design than Lincoln's, and uses interesecting arches, perhaps for the first time in window tracery.

Between the back of the Neville Screen and the Chapel of Nine Altars lies the body of St Cuthbert under a plain grey slab of 1541 with his name on it, a modest memorial to the most modest of saints, but very different from the medieval shrine which it replaced.

Retracing one's steps to the west, the cloister is reached from the south side of the nave. Here is the earliest work at Durham: the undercroft of the refectory belongs to the time of Bishop Walcher, who died in 1080. The chapter house was built about 1140, though the eastern apse was demolished in the eighteenth century, and only rebuilt in 1895. In the west range, the dormitory contains the cathedral museum – though some of the pieces displayed there at the time of writing, including the objects associated with St Cuthbert, are due to be moved to the new Treasury. Here are gravestones from Saxon times onwards, fascinating collections of manuscripts, and early crosses. The splendid kitchen with its unique, rather Islamic vault, was completed in 1370 by John Lewyn, who designed the cloisters and had a hand at least in the design of the Neville Screen.

Re-entering the cathedral, the visitor can complete his tour by turning west, and looking at the west window, a lovely flowing composition of 1337. Near one's feet, on the floor just east of the font, is a marble slab, which once marked the furthest point to the east permitted to women in the cathedral, a restriction imposed by the antipathy to women alleged to have been felt by St Cuthbert.

Finally, at the west end is the Galilee Chapel, built by Richard Wolveston for Bishop Pudsey about 1175. This is also rather Islamic in style, the mosque-like effect produced by four parallel arcades, and originally even more striking before Cardinal Langley, in the fifteenth century, added the pairs of sandstone shafts to strengthen the existing pairs of detached Purbeck ones which supported the arches. Langley also added the external buttressing which prevented the chapel collapsing down the cliff, and blocked the east wall, the original west doorway to the cathedral, in order to place his own tomb against it. This is the large tomb. The more modest affair belongs to one of the great men of the English church, the Saxon historian Bede. Fragments of wall painting survive, all the more easily seen because the large, later windows, contain clear glass.

The exterior of the cathedral can be examined from Palace Green to the north, and, less easily, from College Green to the south. Although the details have mostly been renewed by Wyatt, Scott, and others, it is still enjoyable. The windows with inventive flowing tracery represent what was there before, and the Norman stages of the west towers are authentic. How high they were meant to be is uncertain. There is a corbel table at the top of the Norman work, but it seems likely that this marked a temporary halt to the work, as they can hardly have been intended to finish below the level of the roof ridge. Work continued in thirteenth-century Gothic, and the towers were originally spired. Now they end in pierced parapets and pinnacles added at the end of the eighteenth century.

The crossing tower was built about 1460 by Thomas Barton, and raised to its present height about 1490 by John Bell. It, too, was intended to carry a spire, which was actually begun early in the sixteenth century, and considered again by Wyatt. Fortunately,

nothing came of it. It was bold to raise the tower to its present height on an early Norman crossing. To add a spire, though Norwich got away with it on its original Norman tower, would have been pushing one's luck to put it mildly, and it would have been tragic if the hubristic ambition of later generations had brought ruin to one of the finest Romanesque buildings in existence.

Special Occasions

20 March – St Cuthbert's Day – Procession to tomb of St Cuthbert, with special music and Festal Evensong.

Good Friday – Durham Council of Churches' United Service at the end of a procession through the city.

27 May – Venerable Bede – Procession to Bede's tomb; special music and Festal Evensong.

May or June – Annual Festival of the Friends of the Cathedral – the choir sings from the tower after evensong.

July – The Diocesan Choirs' Festival.

July – Miners' Gala Day Festival Service.

Last Wednesday in October – Commemoration of Founders and Benefactors – Procession of University, City, and Clergy.

Ely

The great Fenland monastery of Ely – founded by St Etheldreda in 673, and refounded as a Benedictine monastery by St Ethelwold in 970 – became a cathedral in 1109. Rebuilding on the grand scale lasted from 1083 until well into the thirteenth century. The plan was a fairly traditional Anglo-Norman one: cruciform, with apsed choir, a lantern tower over the crossing, and a long nave but a single-towered westwork.

The westwork, which still dominates the cathedral, now looks very different from when it was completed about 1200: the north-west transept collapsed in the fifteenth century and was only replaced by buttresses; the original stone spire of *c* 1230 was replaced by an octagonal drum in the fourteenth century; the roof-pitch of the south-west transept was lowered in the late Middle Ages;

and alterations were made to the west portal of the galilee in the nineteenth century.

Entering via the west porch, one is immediately struck by the grandeur of the Norman nave, begun about 1110. It was never vaulted, and its present ceiling is a nineteenth-century reconstruction, painted by LeStrange and Gambier Parry about 1860. From either end one is strongly conscious of the tunnel-like effect caused by its great thirteen-bay length in relation to its width, but from anywhere inside the nave, the large openings at all three levels (the proportions of arcade: gallery: clerestory are 6:5:4) give a liberating sense of light and space.

In the nave is a connection with the founding of the monastery: the plain base and shaft of a cross with an inscription saying that it was given by Etheldreda's steward, Ovin.

Ely is as much a storehouse of Victorian glass as Canterbury is of medieval glass, but little of it is by the best makers: nothing by Morris or Powell, and little by Hardman. The west window, however, is earlier, and dates from the first decade of the nineteenth century.

The transepts are earlier than the nave. Abbot Simeon, who began the rebuilding in 1083, was a brother of Walkelin of Winchester, and it is not surprising to find similarities between their two churches, though only the transepts are available for comparison. Both had east and west aisles; both had low walls dividing the chapels on the east sides; both had a sacristy contrived in the west aisle on the south side – and so one could go on. The most interesting original feature of the Ely transepts is the carving of the capitals of the east arcade on the south side. The roofs are now fine examples of fifteenth-century timber construction, with hammer-beams supported by angels. The north transept has some good Victorian glass by Moore.

The most famous feature of Ely, and one of the wonders of medieval building, is the octagon. Its visual effect is intensely dramatic, allowing a well of light to fall into the heart of the cathedral in a way no ordinary square lantern could do: the octagon has twice as many windows, catching the light from every direction. The opening out of the central area by lopping a bay off choir, nave, and transepts adds to the sense of floating space, an achievement as arresting in its way as the great domes of Byzantium. One catches no reminiscences of it in subsequent British cathedrals until the Metropolitan Cathedral at Liverpool and Clifton in our own day.

The collapse of the crossing tower in 1321 brought down most of the choir with it. The most notable feature of the rebuilding is the gallery, with delicate flowing tracery in the arches. The choir stalls, which originally stood in the octagon, also belong to the repair work, probably designed by William Hurley and completed just after 1340. Scott had the upper canopies filled with carved scenes, which has not helped their general appearance.

Sixty of the seats have misericords.

The presbytery was added to the Norman choir between 1234 and 1252. The connections at this stage were with Lincoln rather than Winchester: just as the west tower of Ely anticipates the Lincoln towers in certain of its details, so the Ely presbytery seems to have been executed by the same school of masons between the time the Lincoln nave was vaulted, about 1234, and the beginning of the Angel Choir there in 1256.

There are some interesting monuments in the north chancel aisle, including one to Bishop Nigellus, 1169, a Tournai marble slab showing the bishop's soul held in a napkin by a large angel, finely carved, and with an architectural surround. It has a dignity absent from a good deal of later sculpture. Bishops Northwold, 1254, and Kilkenny, 1257 have beautiful monuments in Purbeck, and there are some fragments of the shrine of St Etheldreda.

At the east end are two exceptional chantry chapels, Bishop Alcock's on the north side, and Bishop West's on the south. Alcock's is one of the richest pieces of late Gothic in Britain, begun in 1488, thirteen years before the bishop died. It has a fan vault with a pendant, and the south and west sides are incredibly thickly encrusted with canopy work. Bishop West's, made in 1532–3, shortly before his death, is simpler, but has splendid iron gates, delightful sculptural details, and a subtle vault in which gothic and renaissance motifs are mixed. Such sugar-icing gothic as is found in these two chapels is not common in late medieval England, though it occurs elsewhere, in Spain and Portugal for example, and in the Roslin Chapel near Edinburgh. In England it was characteristic rather of the 1320s and 1330s, as the Lady Chapel will show.

The south chancel aisle contains some interesting monuments too, but none as good as the best on the north side. Bishop de Luda's (1299) would have been were it not so damaged.

The Lady Chapel is accessible from the

The interior of the Octagon

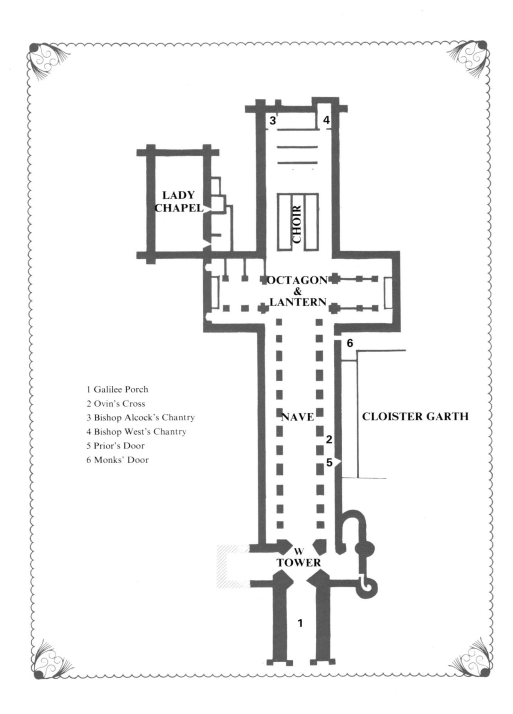

3 Bishop Alcock's Chantry
4 Bishop West's Chantry

LADY
CHAPEL

CHOIR

OCTAGON
&
LANTERN

6

1 Galilee Porch
2 Ovin's Cross
3 Bishop Alcock's Chantry
4 Bishop West's Chantry
5 Prior's Door
6 Monks' Door

NAVE

CLOISTER GARTH

2

5

W
TOWER

1

north transept, but so distinct is it, almost like a separate church, that it is best to leave it until last. Its foundations were laid in 1321, but the fall of the crossing tower delayed operations until about 1335. It has a wonderful undulating series of seating niches along the walls, with nodding ogee canopies and a multitude of rich, albeit damaged carving of the East Midland School. The window tracery is still flowing, except for the later east window inserted in the 1370s, which has moved towards the Perpendicular style. The chapel is roofed by a lierne vault, the most elaborate at Ely; when all this stonework was painted and the windows contained their stained glass, the effect must have been gorgeous. No wonder the reformers and puritans hated it so much. Virtually every sculptured figure has been decapitated.

The cloister is on the south side. It was reached by two of the best twelfth-century doorways in Britain, though the western one, the Prior's Door, now leads only to a small open space, for the cloisters have been much ruined and altered. This and the Monks' Door further east date from about 1135, and are very richly carved. The work has affinities with Burgundy and North Italy.

Finally, two features of the exterior should not be missed, one major and one minor. The minor one is the alteration to the masonry of part of the north transept in 1699 by Grumbold, in consultation with his former master, Sir Christopher Wren. The major one is the outside of the octagon. In its present form even more of the exterior than of the interior is Scott's, but enough is authentic to give a clear indication of the design, especially the rather Spanish quality of the very wide, spreading stone tower below the timberwork. The stonework is more of a square tower with chamfered corners than a regular octagon like the timberwork. One feels somehow that the timber structure should have been capped by a timber spire.

Many of the monastic buildings survive, partly because of the needs of the post-Reformation clergy, but more because of their use by the King's School. The finest of these is Prior Crauden's Chapel, whose building was probably interrupted by the fall of the crossing tower, and completed about 1325. It has niches like those in the Lady Chapel, some unique window tracery, and a fine tile-mosaic pavement.

Prior Crauden's Chapel

Exeter

Exeter Cathedral was founded in 1050. The Norman rebuilding began about 1110, and, as usual, nothing of the Saxon cathedral is left.

The most arresting feature of the exterior is the pair of towers forming transepts, begun about 1133. However, in spite of the blank arcading of the upper parts, they are fairly austere, and would have looked far more impressive with their original timber caps or spires than they do with their present battlements and pinnacles.

Not much is known of the rest of the Norman church, but bomb damage in 1942 brought to light in the nave walling capitals

which suggest that the nave had huge cylindrical columns of the Gloucester-Tewkesbury kind.

Nearly all the rest of the cathedral was built between 1275 and 1375. The west front, of course, belongs to the end of this building programme, and its screen, by William Joy, was completed about 1346. Like most English west fronts outside Yorkshire, it is not entirely successful. The trouble is, it tails away to nothing at the sides, a fact emphasized by the way the nave gable and the aisle roofs form a great triangle. Having said this, one must sympathise with the designer, Thomas Witney, one of the great names in

The West Front

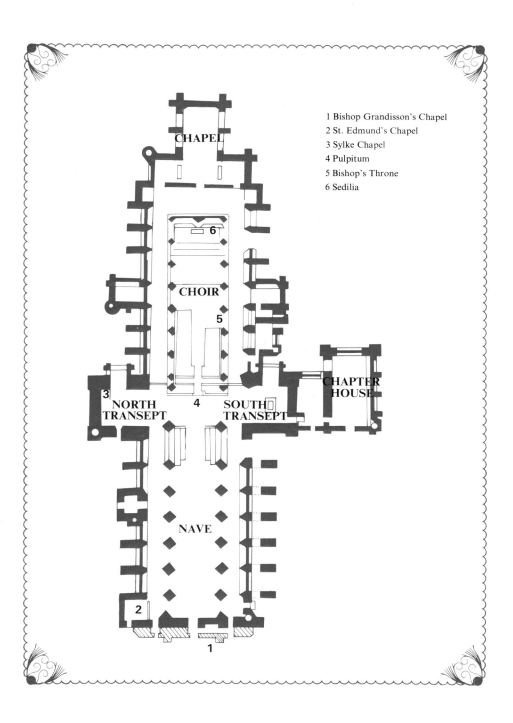

CHAPEL

1 Bishop Grandisson's Chapel
2 St. Edmund's Chapel
3 Sylke Chapel
4 Pulpitum
5 Bishop's Throne
6 Sedilia

6

CHOIR

5

NORTH
TRANSEPT

3

4

SOUTH
TRANSEPT

CHAPTER
HOUSE

NAVE

2

1

English medieval architecture, for towers, or even turrets, would have looked very awkward in the face of the transeptal ones behind. Also, Joy's screen has to be visualized coloured.

The great west window is highly original. Much use is made of quatrefoils and spheric triangles. (The gable window above is also a spheric triangle.) The canopies of the niches in the aisle west walls and the gables of the pinnacles also underline the triangular theme. Most of the figures in the screen are original. The doorways, as so often, especially in the west, are insignificant in scale, but the south one in particular has some nice sculptural detail.

If one has doubts about the west front, they are completely dispelled on entry. Seldom does an English cathedral present such a unified picture as this. Witney, who designed the nave, took over the design of the east end with a minimum of alteration; the general effect is often described as palm-tree-like, but in many ways it is more like a great avenue of beeches. The effect is produced by the brilliant harmony between the shafts of the piers, the mouldings of the arches, and the ribs of the vault. The triforium, which contains the famous minstrels' gallery, is reduced to a narrow band. The vault, which goes on unaltered through into the chancel, scarcely interrupted by the towerless crossing, is one of the finest tierceron vaults in existence.

The screen to St Edmund's Chapel in the north-west corner of the nave is part of the original furnishing. The font of white marble is a late seventeenth-century piece, and in the north aisle is the memorial to the officers and men of the Ninth Lancers, 1860, with two mounted bronze figures.

The pulpitum was put in during the 1320s, that period when stone sculpture sometimes achieves an almost Islamic delicacy of ornament. Also by Thomas Witney, it is of the verandah type, and has altars on the north and south sides. The paintings in the parapet belong to the seventeenth century.

Finally, before leaving the nave, the

The pulpitum

bosses in the vault, especially towards the west end, are of splendid quality, and the tracery of the aisle windows and the clerestory is inventive and interesting. Spheric triangles again appear, and circles are filled with a variety of motifs, all of them attractive.

Architecturally, the transepts are not very interesting – except for the fourteenth-century balconies on the west walls inserted in place of a triforium, and supported on little vaults. The north transept contains the late fourteenth-century clock (redecorated in 1760), the Sylke Chapel (a chantry of 1508 with a gruesome cadaver), and, above it, a late fifteenth-century wall painting of the Ascension.

The chancel was completed before 1309, though, as we have seen, the style was kept so uniform as work proceeded westwards that it looks hardly earlier than the nave. To see development one has to look at the details.

What one is in fact doing as one walks eastwards in this cathedral is to walk slowly back in time. The window tracery of the chancel aisles shows the period of experiment away from pure geometrical forms of early bar-tracery towards the flowing curves of the fourteenth-century work further west. The corbels in the presbytery are superlatively carved: those on the north with naturalistic foliage reminiscent of the Southwell chapter house; those on the south with more conventional bands of foliage more typical of the fourteenth century. The east window of the presbytery is a replacement of 1389.

The chancel is magnificently furnished. The choir stalls are good work of Scott's, dating from the 1870s, but the misericords are thirteenth century, older than the chancel itself, and the earliest set remaining in England. The bishop's throne was designed by John of Glaston and Thomas Witney in 1313. It is the finest in Britain, and among the finest in Europe, with splendid pinnacle work. The sedilia, also by Witney, are a few years younger, and have the rich lushness characteristic of the period of sugar-icing Gothic at its prettiest, but saved from mere prettiness by the strength of the underlying design. If these and the pulpitum are really by Witney, the master of the nave architecture, it seems that his, or his clients', desire to keep the nave in harmony with the early work engendered a restraint that was unnecessary in the furnishings. Similar furnishings, however, are to be found in the Bristol-Tewkesbury-Gloucester area, and the whole story may well never be known. The brass eagle is a typical East Anglian late fifteenth-century piece, hollow, and possibly used as a collecting box.

The Lady Chapel is the earliest part of the rebuilding begun by Bishop Branscombe about 1275. Here there is still stiff-leaf foliage in the piscina and sedilia, but naturalistic foliage in the roof bosses and corbels. Indeed, Exeter is one of the best places in England to study the development of ornamental foliage, a study which need not be in the least academic, so enjoyable is the carving, much of it now repainted and regilded.

A sketch of a wood carving in the Lady Chapel

There are many monuments in the chancel aisles and Lady Chapel. Two of the most interesting belong to those bishops before Grandisson most concerned with the rebuilding. Bishop Branscombe, 1280, who began it, lies between the Lady Chapel and the south-east chapel. His beautifully carved tomb is of basalt. To the north is the much later Bishop Stafford, 1419; both lie under identical canopies of the 1440s. Bishop Stapledon, the other building bishop, died in 1326 and his canopied tomb is to the north of the high altar. Opposite lies his brother, Sir Richard, cross-legged, and with two pages at his feet, one of them holding a horse. Those who like brasses will enjoy those to Sir Peter Courtenay, 1409, in the north chancel aisle, and Canon Langton, 1413, in the north chancel chapel. This chancel chapel and the one opposite contains some thirteenth-century grisaille glass.

The close suffered in the war, but still contains some interesting buildings dating from medieval to Victorian times, of which the Quadrangle, medieval and seventeenth century, is perhaps the best.

Glasgow

Kentigern – usually known by his pet-name, Mungo – set up a monastery at Glasgow towards the end of the seventh century. This monastery, in traditional Celtic fashion, was also the home of the bishop – normally one of the monks. The diocese was loose in area – covering the Kingdom of Strathclyde, which at one time extended as far south as Cumberland and Westmorland. The see was reorganised by David I, and the first cathedral proper was completed in 1136, though nothing of this building survives. In 1508 Glasgow was made an archbishopric, but when episcopacy was abolished in Scotland the cathedral became a parish church.

The cathedral fabric belongs to the Department of the Environment, so the cathedral is at the same time both a working building and an official Ancient Monument.

Desperately unfortunate both in its surroundings and as the prey of early Victorian restoration, Glasgow has still been luckier than almost every other medieval Scottish cathedral in that it has never been allowed to fall into ruin.

The usual approach is from the west, and on first sight the cathedral, black with industrial grime, appears to be a Victorian building: the west front a piece of dull, correct work of 1850, replacing an unusual one with two contrasting towers.

Since 1848, the crossing steeple has provided the only vertical accent. The tower belongs to the late fourteenth century, and the spire was added by Bishop Lauder about 1420. It is 220ft high, recessed behind the parapet, but broached. The two strong bands of ornament give it something of a central European appearance.

Before going in, it is worth walking round to the south side – since this will explain some unusual features inside. Firstly, the transept does not project beyond the line of the aisles, a French custom which gives the cathedral a very compact appearance. Secondly, the ground slopes away sharply to

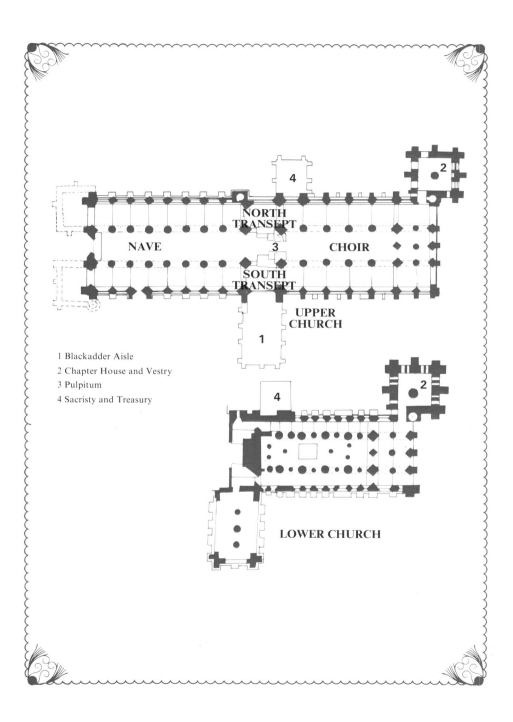

4

2

NORTH
TRANSEPT

NAVE

3

CHOIR

SOUTH
TRANSEPT

UPPER
CHURCH

1

1 Blackadder Aisle
2 Chapter House and Vestry
3 Pulpitum
4 Sacristy and Treasury

2

4

LOWER CHURCH

the east, and the chancel is seen to be constructed in two distinct storeys, which provide an Upper and a Lower Church, the latter of which is a sort of super-crypt. Thirdly, attached to the south transept is an obviously later and unfinished building. This is the 'aisle' (the word in Scotland tends to retain its older meaning of 'wing') begun by Bishop Blackadder at the end of the fifteenth century, but of which only the crypt was built. Finally, walking round to the east end, a strange building with stepped gables is appended to the north-east corner: this is the chapter house and vestry.

Inside, the nave impresses at once by its restraint and simplicity. At first sight it looks thirteenth century, but the pier-bases and capitals are impossible for that date, and in fact it was added in the fourteenth century in a style which took great pains to blend with the earlier work further east.

In the centre window of the north aisle is glass by Douglas Strachan, one of the leading designers in Scotland this century, depicting the life of Moses. The deep blues and greens are characteristic of his work. Much of the other glass belongs to the period 1938–58, while some is Victorian. The pulpitum dates from about 1420. It is a particularly solid piece, with a wide gallery, and an unusually depressed arch for its period.

From the south transept one can descend into the Blackadder Aisle. This is in the somewhat heavy-handed style usual in late medieval Scotland, but the upper storey was doubtless intended to be lighter and more graceful. The capitals and bosses have interesting carving, including a good deal of naturalistic leaf work.

Retracing one's steps to the pulpitum, one reaches the finest part of the cathedral, the Higher and Lower Kirks at the east end. A little work here survives from about 1200, but this grand conception is essentially of the time of Bishop William de Bondington, 1233–58, and completed by about 1270 at the latest.

Both churches have the same plan: a central vessel with side-aisles and a further aisle at the east end containing four chapels accessible from the ambulatory.

The chancel 'nave' is not vaulted. The present timber roof represents its predecessor and includes some fifteenth century ribs and bosses. The aisles and chapels all have stone vaults, with excellent bosses, mostly thirteenth century, but some dating from later medieval repair work. St Lawrence's Chapel, the southernmost of the four, is encumbered by the huge monument to Archbishop Law, 1632, built during Charles I's revival of episcopacy.

On the north side, the sacristy was added in the fifteenth century by Bishop Cameron, and still has its original oak door from the chancel aisle. Further east, the chapter house upper room is also accessible from this aisle. It was reconstructed about 1420–30.

The Lower Church is entered by the steps near the pulpitum. The central vessel is the Lady Chapel, and the alternate large piers correspond to the piers in the chancel above. Here lay the tomb of St Kentigern, and, immediately above, behind the high altar in the Upper Kirk, would have stood his shrine. The capitals in the Lower Kirk are beautifully carved with stiff-leaf foliage and figures. In the south aisle a few fragments of the shrine can be seen, as well as numerous effigies, tombs, and architectural fragments of minor importance. The only one that matters is Bishop Wishart, 1316, whose effigy still lies in its original place at the east end. In the north aisle are the entrances to the thirteenth-century lower floor of the chapter house, and the treasury, beneath the sacristy.

Special Occasions

13 January – St Kentigern's Day – Preacher usually the Moderator of the General Assembly of the Church of Scotland
May – 2nd or 3rd Sunday – Kirking of the Lord Provost, Bailies, and Councillors of the City District Council.
October – Annual Seafarers' Service.
October – Kirking of the Deacon Convener of the Trades of Glasgow, with the fourteen incorporated trades represented.

Gloucester

The monastery of St Peter at Gloucester was founded late in the seventh century. It was Benedictine from 1022 until the Dissolution, when Henry VIII made its church the cathedral of a new diocese. The Norman rebuilding began under Abbot Serlo in 1089, and was completed by about 1120. A great deal of this church still stands, though some of it is hidden under later remodelling.

The Lower Severn/Bristol Channel area was one of great architectural adventurousness in the Middle Ages: twelfth-century Wells did much to create English Gothic; Bristol, about 1300, is one of its most exciting descendants; and Gloucester spans them,

with experimental but not entirely successful early twelfth-century work on the one hand, and work of the 1330s on the other which was to exercise a powerful influence on English architecture for two hundred years.

Externally Gloucester is a finely proportioned church. Like most western cathedrals it is fairly compact, and with its 225ft crossing tower, it shows nothing of the long low profile so common further east. Even at a glance it is clearly a grand building, and we can be grateful that a Puritan plan to pull it down came to nothing.

Entrance is by the south porch, built about 1420, but heavily restored in the

nineteenth century when the present figures were inserted. This formed part of a proposed remodelling of the nave, begun after the collapse of the Norman west front, but abandoned after the first two bays. The south aisle had already been rebuilt a century earlier – see the ballflower ornament on the vault and on the windows with their butterfly tracery—as its predecessor was showing signs of failure.

The rest of the nave is solidly Norman. The north aisle retains its original rib-vault, though the high vault belongs to the mid thirteenth century. The nave is very similar to nearby Tewkesbury, and its strangeness lies in the repudiation of usual Norman proportions, which, as we shall see, had been used further east. The arcade has huge cylindrical piers which seem altogether too massive for the arches, their size accentuated by their small moulded capitals, and by the tiny triforium above them. The effect is oppressive, almost ugly, and one sympathises with Abbot Morwent's desire to replace it in the fifteenth century.

The pulpit, lectern, and organ case are good seventeenth-century work. Of the many monuments, three in the south aisle and two in the north are particularly worth seeing. In the north aisle these are to Sarah Morley, 1784, by Flaxman, and Canon Tinling, 1897, by Henry Wilson. In the south aisle they are to a fifteenth-century knight and lady, to Ellys, Bishop of St Davids, 1761, and to Dame Mary Strachan, 1770.

The south transept assures Gloucester of a niche in architectural history. Court architects in London had moved towards a new style a little before this, with a tendency to run mullions up to the heads of arches, though their work at St Stephen's Chapel, Westminster, and the chapter house at Old St Paul's is now known only from prints. But it was the designer of the south window of this transept who developed it into what we know as Perpendicular, a style which took a generation or more to catch on everywhere, but which, when it did, revolutionized and very nearly standardized English Gothic until the Reformation. The window was put in

about 1335, but the transept was not rebuilt, only remodelled. It was completed by an early lierne vault, but the most striking feature of the elevation is the interference with it from the huge flying buttresses of the tower descending visibly through its structure – a feature borrowed from Worcester. In this transept is a fine monument to Abraham and Gertrude Blackleech, 1639.

The crossing is also an exciting piece of architecture. Like the transept it is Norman in its bones, but altered in the fourteenth and fifteenth centuries. The flattish arches under the main ones are not strainers such as may be found at Wells or Salisbury. In their form they are a much more elegant version of the Bristol choir aisles, but they are there simply to make the complicated lierne vault structurally possible.

The north transept is similar to the south but later, being remodelled about 1370. It contains an early thirteenth-century Purbeck-embellished screen, and a superb clock case by Henry Wilson of 1903.

Now down into the crypt. This groin-vaulted room with its three aisles and stumpy

Angel bosses on the choir vault

Earlier plans for twin towers were abandoned, but an ambitious decorative scheme was started, using polychrome stonework. The walls were built in alternate courses of red and white sandstone. The doorways were given special treatment: in the northern and central doorways the orders of voussoirs are alternately red and white, giving an effect of concentric rings; in the south doorway, red and white stone is used for alternate voussoirs in each order, giving a spiky, radiating effect; and the contemporary south transept doorway provides another variation on the theme, a chequer pattern. The inspiration for all this may well have been the strikingly similar late twelfth-century west front of Le Puy Cathedral, at the start of one of the pilgrimage routes to Compostela. At Kirkwall, however, the work was not completed, and when work was resumed later in the Middle Ages, the polychrome work was abandoned in favour of a simple, rather austere design.

It is apparent on entering the nave that it is not all of a piece. The west end belongs to the time of the completion of the front; the main part, still Romanesque in character, belongs to the late twelfth century; and the easternmost section, with scalloped capitals, belongs to the original work. The rib-vaulted aisles have blank arcading springing from twin shafts, a popular Anglo-Norman feature. Originally a wooden ceiling was intended, but about 1200 the decision was taken to provide a high vault. Since the nave was not yet completed, and closed to the west merely by a partition wall, this decision came close to causing disaster: the west bays were pushed westwards by the thrust of the vault and the pillars still lean noticeably. The west section of the vault was removed as a safety measure, and was not replaced when the nave was completed.

The crossing was reconstructed about 1200. It was a tricky operation involving the replacement, not merely the encasement, of the piers and arches and the arches to the aisles. It seems that the familiar problem of settlement and outward thrust had threatened disaster.

Immediately adjacent parts of the gallery and clerestory were also rebuilt, but otherwise all round the crossing is what is left of Rognvald's cathedral. The transepts have no aisles, and therefore did not have the buttressing necessary if a high vault had been intended. Their eastern chapels were planned with apses, but completed about 1200 with square ends.

As work began from the east, the oldest parts now left to us are the western bays of the choir. They are very similar to the east end of the nave with their cylindrical piers, scalloped capitals, and triple-stepped arches. The gallery openings are not subdivided, but alternation of different coloured stone is used in the voussoirs. There is a subdued use of ornament – billet and sawtooth in the arcade, nook-shafts in the clerestory – and the whole elevation is standard Anglo-Norman, dignified, but without inspiration.

Early in the thirteenth century, Rognvald's apse was pulled down, and the usual lengthening and squaring of the chancel took place. This new work is the most beautiful in the cathedral, and the piers and capitals are particularly interesting. The piers are compound, consisting of an octagonal core, with keeled shafts on the cardinal faces, and pairs of shafts in the diagonals which seem to flow into the hollow which separates them. Some of the capitals have French crockets while others have English stiff-leaf – with plenty of engaging little figures among the foliage, including one of the female fertility figures known as sheila-na-gigs. It seems probable that French and English masons worked side by side, and the architect may well have been a Frenchman.

The arches are richly moulded, and the east window is a fine composition with a tracery wheel in the arch head. The mullions subdividing the lancets are a later medieval insertion. The high vault is quadripartite with a longitudinal ridge-rib of English inspiration, and fine vaulting shafts.

As usual in Scotland, no ancient furnishings have survived except for three early sixteenth-century bells. A few oak panels probably belong to late sixteenth-century pews. One or two medieval tombs survive, though the remains of the two saints associated with the foundation of the cathedral, Magnus and Rognvald, were discovered earlier this century hidden in cavities in pillars in the choir. There are some pleasantly discreet post-Reformation memorials, with none of the arrogance in death of contemporary English gentry, and, indeed, the great charm of the interior of Kirkwall is the lack of clutter which would have been disastrous in so small a building.

Returning now to the outside, the tower was completed late in the Middle Ages, but the spire was destroyed by lightning in 1671, and replaced by the pyramidal cap seen in old prints. The present spire is early twentieth century.

Two more doorways to notice are those on either side of the nave. The north doorway is a fine piece of work of about 1200: shafted, with stiff-leaf capitals, a round arch, and a fine, steeply pitched shallow porch whose sole purpose was to give depth to recess the entrance in a series of orders. It has a strange lozenge-shaped niche in the gable head. The south doorway was inserted shortly before the Reformation; its head consists of three sides of a hexagon instead of an arch.

Just to the south of the cathedral lie the remains of the Bishop's and the Earl's Palaces, and to the south west stands Tankerness House. All these buildings are largely sixteenth century, and make a delightful ensemble. Indeed, Kirkwall is a cathedral that deserves to be far better known.

Nave, Looking East—from a 19th century print

Lincoln

There was a bishop's see in Lindsey in the seventh century, but with the onset of the Danish invasions it was moved first to Leicester and then to Dorchester-on-Thames. In 1073, after the Council of Windsor had decreed that bishops' seats should henceforth be in walled towns, Bishop Remigius moved his cathedral back again to the north of his unwieldy diocese, which stretched from the Humber to the Thames. He chose the Roman city of Lincoln, standing high above the Witham on an oolitic limestone ridge, easily defensible, and, by eleventh-century standards, with excellent road and river communications. We can be grateful for his choice which gave rise to one of the most dramatic of English cathedrals.

Ideally visitors should approach from the south, by walking up the Strait and then Steep Hill, a strenuous ascent, but one which gives, as nowhere else in Britain except perhaps Iona, a sense of the fulfilment of a pilgrimage. The cathedral is overwhelming, a vast building with nothing in uphill Lincoln to rival its dominance.

At the top of Steep Hill the castle lies to the west and the cathedral to the east. One approaches the cathedral through the fourteenth-century Exchequer Gate, a reminder that the precinct was once a walled city within a walled city. There were originally six gates, but the only other survivor is the more modest Pottergate to the north-east.

Walking through the Exchequer Gate, one is immediately confronted by all that remains of Remigius's church, now the kernel of a much altered and extended west front. The five stepped giant niches, embedded in a vast area of plain wall – the only plain wall surface in the whole building – give strong contrasts of light and shade, very different in effect from the Gothic arcading of the rest of the front. Nothing could demonstrate more clearly the difference between the way the late eleventh century and the mid thirteenth century handled wall surfaces.

The three principal hollows may hint at what once lay behind them, for they look very

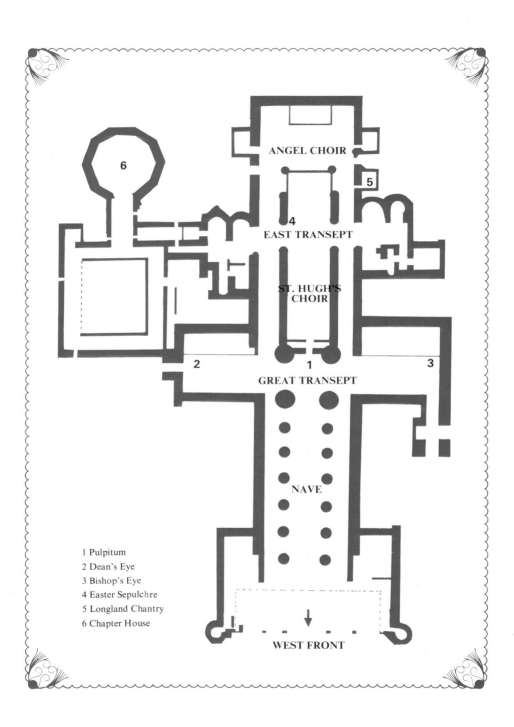

ANGEL CHOIR

5

4

EAST TRANSEPT

6

ST. HUGH'S
CHOIR

2   1   3

GREAT TRANSEPT

NAVE

1 Pulpitum
2 Dean's Eye
3 Bishop's Eye
4 Easter Sepulchre
5 Longland Chantry
6 Chapter House

WEST FRONT

much like a section cut through nave and aisles, telling of a tall, narrow building of somewhat Saxon proportions, though certainly of far more than Saxon size. Towers were built, or at any rate started, where the present ones are, that is, set back from the front which was therefore always intended as a screen.

Remigius's cathedral was not destined to last long in its original form. It was damaged by fire in 1124, and again, by a much more serious fire in 1141. After this, Bishop Alexander had to embark on a major restoration. Once more, what little is left of his work is to be found at the west front.

In spite of the civil war that was still intermittently raging, the new work shows knowledge of the most up-to-date continental style. Alexander replaced the original portals by the present ones, carved with all the opulence then coming into fashion. The outer shafts of the central doorway have geometrical decoration reminiscent of the Durham piers on a miniature scale. The three inner orders have a rich variety of trails and medallions with beasts, birds, monsters, and human figures. All three portals have 'beakheads' – a series of animal heads biting on a roll-moulding; and the hood-mould of the central portal, now cut into by the range of fourteenth-century canopied statues above, has dragon mask terminals. At the same time as the statues were added, a window was inserted into each of the three largest niches, giving much-needed light inside, but spoiling the austere original conception outside.

The lowest tier of interlaced blank arcading also belongs to Bishop Alexander's work – as do the sculptured friezes at the north and south ends of the façade. On the south side are scenes from the early chapters of Genesis, interrupted by a contemporary Daniel in the Lions' Den; and on the north side are Dives and Lazarus, followed by the joys of the blessed, the harrowing of hell, and the torments of the damned. Thus the twelfth-century worshipper was confronted by the sobering themes of sin, judgment, and salvation even before he entered the building.

Inside, the only relics of the Norman cathedral are to be found in the nave. Both are of Flemish workmanship in Tournai marble. One is the large font with its grotesque carvings, dating from Alexander's time; the other is a tomb slab with a Tree of Jesse instead of an effigy. It was said to be Remigius's, damaged by falling timber in the fire of 1124, but most scholars now regard it as belonging to later in the twelfth century.

Alexander's cathedral, like Remigius's, was short-lived. An earthquake of 1185 rent it from top to bottom. Everything except the west front had to be demolished, and rebuilding began in 1192. The bishop at the time, Hugh of Avalon, was a Carthusian monk, but, severe though the Carthusian rule was, their churches had none of the puritanism associated with the early Cistercians, and there was probably no dissension between St Hugh and his Dean and Chapter when they chose as master mason a man of powerful but eccentric genius. It is not known for certain whether this man was Geoffrey of Noiers or Richard Mason, for both names appear in connection with the new work, but the usual convention of attributing the work to Geoffrey will be followed here.

The new architect used a Gothic style as pure in its way as that of Wells. The east end was replaced later, but the choir, the east transepts, and part of the main transepts are his, and were probably completed after St Hugh's death in 1200. Tall, needle-like lancets were used, far longer in relation to their breadth than the windows of Wells or Canterbury, thus setting a fashion that was to prevail in a more exaggerated form for nearly a century in Northern England.

Geoffrey was a restless innovator, He experimented with his vaulting, as can be seen in the rather odd forms to be found in the chapels along the east transepts, and more boldly in the high vault of the choir, where he invented the ridge-rib and the tierceron. Both became normal features of English Gothic, and tiercerons were used throughout Western Europe, but never so strangely as here on their first appearance. Later architects used them to form regular patterns, but in

St Hugh's Choir they are used in a weird lop-sided way – a strange experiment in deliberate asymmetry that nobody ever felt inclined to repeat.

Geoffrey also showed a typical early Gothic indifference to squashed arches or half-arches to end arcading, and would probably be perplexed at our concern for such niceties. But he was capable of achieving real beauty as well as novelty. Look, for example, at the lovely wall-arcading in two rows, one behind the other, so that the arcades overlap to give a sort of three-dimensional version of intersecting arches. The alternation is emphasized by the use of Purbeck shafts for the front row, and limestone for the back.

He was fond of Purbeck, a fashion he may have taken from Canterbury, but he used the slender polished shafts far more extensively, adventurously, and effectively than his predecessors in earlier buildings. The workmanship is all very fine, and the capitals here show stiff-leaf carving at its crispest and best.

The furnishings in this part of the cathedral are all later than the architecture. The stone screens between choir and choir aisles are of various dates between about 1240 and 1310, and the lovely iron grilles at the east crossing were made about the end of the thirteenth century. In the south aisle is the remains of the shrine of Little St Hugh, a local boy said to have been ritually murdered by the Jews in 1255, a story which sounds like a typical piece of medieval anti-semitism. The choir stalls, with their splendid misericords and elbow-rests, were made between 1361 and 1372, though they were extensively restored in late Victorian times.

Visitors who have the time to follow the cathedral's evolution will resist the strong temptation to go further east to the Angel Choir at this stage, but will now go back to the crossing and main transepts. Before looking at the architecture there are some details to attend to which are among the most beautiful things in the cathedral. First, the pulpitum, which was made in the fourteenth century by

the same workshop as the Southwell screen. For sheer quality it is on a par with the roughly contemporary Lady Chapel at Ely. Above it, an interesting contrast, is the Gothic organ case of 1826. To the north and south of the pulpitum are the gateways from the transepts to the choir aisles – made by the same masons who worked on the Angel Choir. Their design and carvings are equally superb.

Geoffrey of Noiers, however, did not complete the main transepts. This was done, mainly in the 1220s and 30s by two other masters, Michael and Alexander. The collapse of the crossing tower in the 1230s probably made little difference, as it may well have been scheduled to come down anyway. Michael and Alexander used the same general scheme as Geoffrey, but with some simpli-fication, a little updating, and fewer eccentricities. The finest feature of this work is the rose window in the north transept called the Dean's Eye, which still contains its original glass. The corresponding south transept window, the Bishop's Eye, had new flowing tracery put in about a century later. It is filled with a kaleidoscope of medieval glass fragments.

In the crossing tower appears a form of decoration found also on its exterior, and on the west front gable – diagonal stone lattice work. Rare in Britain, it is sometimes found on the Continent.

Alexander was almost certainly responsible for the building of the nave. As in Geoffrey's work, there is an interesting contrast between Purbeck and Lincoln stone in the beautifully designed piers, with their delicate shafts surrounding a central core. Indeed, from Geoffrey's time onwards, it is as though that great man's genius earned the undying respect of his followers, who sought to interpret his ideas in the idiom of their own day, and who took them to other cathedrals like Worcester and Ely. Alexander's gallery is richer than Geoffrey's, with triplet instead of twin openings, and more developed plate tracery in the spandrels.

The Angel Choir, as the presbytery is always known, is the climax of Lincoln, and one of the climaxes of English Gothic. It was built between 1255 and 1280 to hold the shrine of St Hugh. It was designed by Simon of Thirsk. Those who know Ely will realise that the presbytery there lies in time between the nave and the Angel Choir here, and it seems possible that Sampson, who designed it, worked with Alexander at Lincoln, and that Simon of Thirsk worked with Sampson at Ely. Simon carefully harmonized the proportions of his work with Geoffrey's, but he worked in a thoroughly up-to-date style. Bar tracery, a French invention, reached England at Binham Priory and Westminster Abbey in the 1240s. Lincoln was perhaps the first English cathedral to use it, a little before Lichfield. The Angel Choir gallery makes the earlier ones look gauche by comparison: it has a logic and an assurance that plate tracery

The Angel Choir

never possessed. But the real possibilities opened up by bar tracery lay in fenestration. Windows could now be far larger than ever before and glazing could become correspondingly more ambitious. In the great east window, Simon took bar tracery far beyond his prototypes and produced a huge eight-light window nearly 60ft high. Its forms are simple – the whole design is based only on arches and circles – but the effect is tremendous. Its glass, by Ward and Hughes, dates from 1855, is pleasant, and wisely makes no attempt to compete with the architecture, while keeping the interior light enough to make the sculptural details easy to enjoy. The angels which give the presbytery its name are in the spandrels of the gallery. Various styles appear in the sculpture; the best are in the style of the censing angels of Westminster Abbey. The Lincoln imp is to be found here too, at the foot of the north-east vaulting shaft. The clerestory is a marvellous composition with the tracery repeated on either side of the wall-passage, giving a three-dimensional effect.

There are plenty of good furnishings in this part of the cathedral. Here there is space only to mention two. One is the fourteenth-century base of the shrine of the head of St Hugh. The other is the Easter sepulchre. Every Good Friday before the Reformation, the host was placed in the breast of a figure of Christ which was then interred in the Easter Sepulchre. From then till Easter morning a candle was kept burning before it, and a vigil was kept by a succession of watchers. On Easter Morning the Host was borne triumphantly forth. This Easter sepulchre, made just before 1300, is one of the earliest known, and is combined with a tomb – a vivid declaration of the unknown donor's belief in the Resurrection. At the base the soldier guards are depicted fast asleep, and the contrast between the sleeping unbelievers and the vigilant faithful will not have escaped the patient watchers. The vaults inside the sepulchre are skeletal, the first known example of flying ribs, soon to appear so dramatically at Bristol.

Returning now to the outside of the

cathedral, the three towers can be compared. The crossing tower, first completed in the 1240s, was raised about 1310. The western towers were raised to their present height in the fifteenth century. The other external feature to note is the south portal of the Angel Choir, which forms a judgment porch of the kind commonly found in France. Though considerably restored, it contains a good deal of original and interesting sculpture deriving from Westminster Abbey. Next to it, the Longland Chantry, 1548, is in the French flamboyant style.

The chapter house, built from about 1220 to 1260, is the first of many polygonal ones which became an English speciality. It may derive from Worcester's round one,

especially if the Alexander who worked at Lincoln and the Alexander who worked at Worcester are one and the same. The cloisters were started towards the end of the thirteenth century.

Otherwise the details of the exterior of Lincoln are not very interesting. There is a surfeit of rather monotonous decoration, but the ensemble, particularly seen obliquely from the south-east or south-west, is splendid. The harmony of its post-Norman parts is as satisfying outside as in, and it is this harmony which makes Lincoln not only one of the most important British cathedrals architecturally, but also one of the most beautiful.

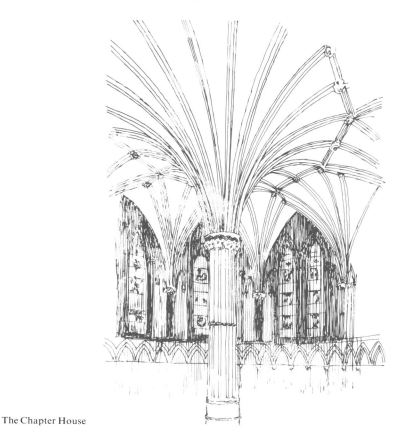

The Chapter House

iverpool (Anglican)

The uniqueness of the city of Liverpool lies in its possession of two major twentieth century cathedrals that lie close enough in space for their crowns to form part of the same skyline, but far enough apart in inspiration for it to be almost unbelievable that they were both being built at the same time.

The Anglican diocese was set up in 1880, and the design for the cathedral accepted in 1903 – when the architect, Giles Gilbert Scott, was only 21.

It is a vast structure, the largest Anglican cathedral in the world, and perhaps the last to be conceived wholly in the medieval spirit and to be built entirely of stone in the Gothic style.

Scott, of course, belonged to the great architectural clan of that name, and it was as inconceivable that he would have designed a cathedral in anything other than Gothic as it was that the chapter would have accepted it if he had. It has, however, proved very expensive to build; it will scarcely be cheap to maintain, and there is a real possibility that in time to come an impoverished Church may regard this beautiful building as a colossal white elephant.

The cathedral is built of local red sandstone from Woolton, and the central tower, easily the best part of the exterior, is 331ft high, 16ft higher than the tip of Norwich's spire. It has octagonal buttresses, and the whole tower turns into an irregular octagon after the first stage. The buttresses finish below the top in a froth of pinnacles, and the main parapet is pinnacled too, somewhat more conventionally. Seen from near or far, it is one of the most impressive towers in England.

The rest of the exterior has immense dignity – its composition an original treatment of a centuries-old theme.

The great sensations of the interior are of height and space, brilliantly achieved. This impression is particularly strong in the unexpected vistas obtained looking into the great central space from the nave bridge and Lady Chapel gallery.

It seems neither new nor old, but somehow suspended in time. If one has to anchor it, then it is best regarded as the last truly great Victorian building in England, even though Scott's original design was made in 1901, the year of the Queen's death.

The way to enjoy it is to wander freely. Nothing of the furnishings is particularly noteworthy, though few visitors will dismiss their impeccable craftsmanship as trivial. Those acquainted with Spanish Gothic will notice the curving ribs of the high vaults, the transverse aisle vaults, and the reredoses. Other details belong as surely to the English tradition. But there is a sense of Gothic anonymity about this building which will appeal to people who find the strongly individual decorative schemes of the Catholic cathedral and Coventry hard to feel at home with.

Special Occasion
May – Commemoration of the Battle of the Atlantic.

iverpool (Roman Catholic)

The Roman Catholic diocese of Liverpool dates from 1850. In 1932 Sir Edwin Lutyens designed a colossal cathedral, larger than Scott's, and work began the following year. It was to have had the largest dome in the world. Admirers of Lutyens' houses will be disappointed that his cathedral was not built. It would doubtless have been a great building, but, like the Anglican one, it looked backwards for inspiration, though in this case to Wren rather than the Middle Ages, and its upkeep would have been prohibitive.

By 1940 the crypt was complete, but the war stopped the work. Rising costs had already put a question mark over its completion, and in 1958 new designs were invited, subject to stringent conditions. One was that the Lutyens crypt should be retained; another was a price limit in 1959 values of £1 million; and a third was that it should be able to seat 3,000 people with an unobscured view of the high altar. Moreover, architects were reminded that the liturgical

trend was to associate the congregation ever more closely with the celebrant of the Mass. The ministers at the altar, they were told, should not be remote figures.

The design chosen was by Sir Frederick Gibberd, and the cathedral was completed in 1967, four and a half years after it was begun, thus taking about half as long as Coventry, and only a fraction of the time taken to build the Anglican cathedral. Affectionately nicknamed the Mersey Funnel, Gibberd's cathedral will surely be ranked by future historians among the masterpieces of British twentieth-century architecture.

It is a centrally planned building with radiating chapels and topped by a soaring crown above the conical roof, 290ft high.

Lutyens' crypt was finished off with a platform for open-air services and the new cathedral rises immediately to the south of it. The chapels are all different in design, thus

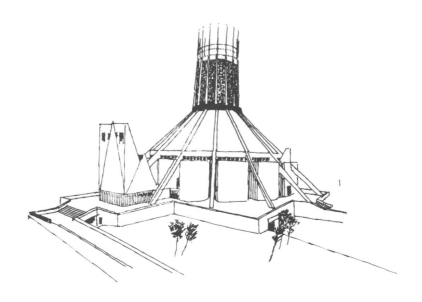

avoiding the monotony of perfect symmetry. The main entrance is below the bell-tower on the south side. The great concrete relief on its face contains the symbolism of the three crosses in a somewhat barbaric idiom; the entrance doors below are of bronze-faced fibre glass with an infilling of concrete, and show the symbols of the four evangelists. Both were designed by William Mitchell. The main structure of the cathedral is of reinforced concrete, with an aluminium-clad roof, but the chapels are of brick, stone-faced.

Inside there is a tremendous impression of space, height, and peace: just like the Anglican cathedral in fact, but the means could scarcely be more different. The dominant factor is the abstract coloured glass. It need not be described in detail, and the visitor can enjoy it for himself, noticing the different colour schemes for each chapel, the blue vertical shafts between them, and the glorious glass of the lantern – by John Piper and Patrick Reyntiens, like the baptistery window at Coventry. What will not be apparent, even so, is that this cathedral contains more glass than any other in the world. The lantern alone has 16 windows, each 65ft high and 12ft wide. Among all its rich colours are three shafts of white light, symbolising the Trinity.

The Blessed Sacrament Chapel is particularly effective, for windows, reredos, and tabernacle were all designed by Ceri Richards. The baptistery has a beautiful simplicity, with a very plain drum-shaped font, and tellingly simple bronze and brass gates designed, like the floor of the cathedral, by David Atkins. The statue of the Virgin in the Lady Chapel is by Robert Brumby.

But what matters here above all is the position of the high altar in the centre of the building, a plain white marble slab from Skopje, with a bronze crucifix by Elizabeth Frink, and, suspended above it, an openwork canopy of linked vertical tubes. It is this centrality of the altar, with the congregation ranged round it, which marks a revolution in British cathedrals. Centrally planned churches have existed before, particularly in the Byzantine east, but the altar was always in an eastern apse, never in the middle. Artistically speaking, Coventry is the first truly modern British cathedral. From the point of view of planning and liturgy the honour belongs to Metropolitan Liverpool – as new in its day as Wells was at the end of the twelfth century. Whether it will beget as large a progeny is doubtful. It seems more likely that the days of cathedral building are nearly done, and that this building foreshadows the end of a centuries old art rather than heralds a new beginning.

Norwich

The building of Norwich cathedral was initiated by Bishop Losinga in 1096 and completed in 1145. In spite of fires in 1171, 1272 (as a result of riots), and 1463 (as a result of lightning) a great deal of the early cathedral still survives. It has a flint core faced with Caen stone: Barnack stone has also been used, and so the stonework – taken from one of the best of English and one of the best of French oolite quarries – is of excellent quality.

Ideally one's first view of the cathedral should be from the east, perhaps from along by the river. The chapel at the extreme east end of the Cathedral was built in 1930. The rest of the chancel belongs to Losinga's church (except for the upper part of the elevation which dates from after the fall of the original spire in 1362).

The nave and transepts are also basically Norman – as is the great crossing tower, one of the few early lanterns to survive. The present spire, 315ft high, was built in the last quarter of the fifteenth century. Although

nearly 100ft lower than Salisbury's, it dominates the cathedral almost equally powerfully – but, since the building lies in a hollow, it has a less dramatic effect on the townscape.

The west front is Norman, but heavily restored by Salvin and with a huge fifteenth-century window. It has neither the impressive-ness of such fronts as Peterborough or Ely, nor the sculpture of, say, Lichfield or Exeter.

Inside, the Norman nave is fourteen bays long – exceptional even for England. The gallery is about as high as the arcade, and its height is emphasized by the lack of subdivision of the arches. The clerestory is also tall, and has the usual triple arches. The lierne vault, with its 270 bosses, dates from about 1460, a finish totally unlike anything the walls were built to support, but very effective in its elaboration against the simplicity of the work below. The strange hole in the vault enabled materials to be winched up from inside during work on the roof. One pier on each side of the nave is

spiral-fluted, Durham style; similar piers were once to be found at Castle Acre Priory not very far away.

The glass in the great west window was made by Hedgeland in 1854 – very old-fashioned in its flowing composition and in its colouring, but infinitely superior to the rows of insipid saints that many glaziers at that time, and, indeed, in the fifteenth century, would have put there instead.

The groined vaults of the aisles reveal the earliness of the work, though two bays on the south side have been altered to provide an elaborate early sixteenth-century chantry for Bishop Nykke. The soffits of the arcade arches have been panelled, and the aisle vaults have been replaced by panelled transverse tunnel vaults. A little further to the east in the south aisle are tantalizing fragments of what must once have been very beautiful wall-painting of about 1175. The effect of such decoration over large areas of the cathedral is now scarcely imaginable.

The choir is situated in the nave, west of the crossing. The stalls are rather a jumble and parts of them are now in the crossing. Those still in the choir have some fine misericords. The lectern, a pelican rather than the usual eagle, is a late fifteenth-century Flemish piece, an unexpected acquisition when one considers that some-where in East Anglia, quite possibly in Norwich itself, was the centre of production of late medieval English lecterns, examples of which can be found as far away as Venice. The eastermost bays of the clerestory have the mock-ashlar painting restored, as has the west wall of the chancel, above the crossing arch.

The crossing tower is an open lantern, as imposing within as without, one of the best Norman towers in England. The transepts are still basically early Norman, rather muddled in their composition, and in parts heavily restored.

The transept vaults are early sixteenth-century insertions, and, like all the other late vaults at Norwich, have a multitude of bosses. In the north transept three monuments are worth picking out: Bishop Bathurst, by

Chantrey, 1841, Bishop Pelham, by Forsyth, 1896, and 'Sweet Vi', Violet Morgan, by Derwent Wood, 1921. The moving inscription on this monument is at the back, and can only be read by leaning up against the wall.

The chancel is extremely impressive, probably more so now than when it was first built, since the fourteenth-century clerestory replacing the one damaged by the fall of the spire is much taller than its predecessor, and the vault, put in after 1472, is similar to the one in the nave. Stylistic purists may be discomfited by this juxtaposition of early Norman and late medieval work, but everyone else will find it very enjoyable. The clerestory glass, by Warrington, 1847, is appropriate, and, indeed, few places can have been luckier in their early Victorian glass than Norwich.

In the apse is the bishop's throne, restored in 1959 to the position it always had in the early church, that is, at the extreme east facing west, and raised up, a much more dramatic site than the customary medieval and modern one on the south side of the chancel. The throne itself is unimpressive, but of great historic interest as two fragments of it may belong to the eighth century, one of them part of the bishop's throne at that time.

The chancel arcade was remodelled by Bishop Goldwell, who built the vault and the spire. His chantry chapel forms part of the composition, and his alabaster effigy is unique in showing the Bishop in cope rather than chasuble.

Leaving the presbytery on the south side, the first chapel one reaches off the south chancel aisle is the Bauchon Chapel of 1330 which contains some splendid bosses illustrating the same story as that told by Chaucer's Man of Lawe, and a modern statue of the Virgin Mary by John Skelton.

Next, as one walks east, comes St Luke's Chapel. It and the Jesus Chapel, in the equivalent position on the north side, contain no straight walls. English medieval architecture was generally obsessed by straight walls, and the subtle interplay of curving surfaces in this eleventh-century

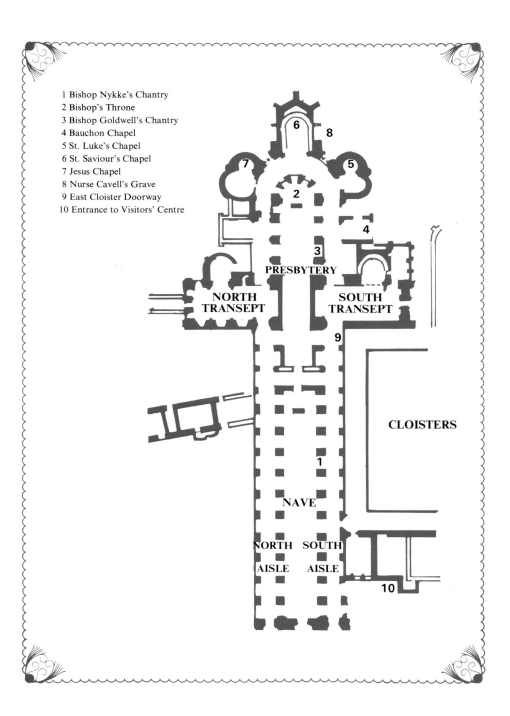

1 Bishop Nykke's Chantry
2 Bishop's Throne
3 Bishop Goldwell's Chantry
4 Bauchon Chapel
5 St. Luke's Chapel
6 St. Saviour's Chapel
7 Jesus Chapel
8 Nurse Cavell's Grave
9 East Cloister Doorway
10 Entrance to Visitors' Centre

6
8
7
5
2
4
3
PRESBYTERY
NORTH TRANSEPT
SOUTH TRANSEPT
9
CLOISTERS
1
NAVE
NORTH AISLE
SOUTH AISLE
10

composition is a welcome change. St Luke's Chapel contains a font illustrating the seven sacraments, with a crucifixion panel on the eighth side. But its finest possession, and arguably the finest in the whole cathedral is the retable, given by Bishop Despenser about 1380. It has five panels showing, from left to right, the flagellation, Christ bearing his cross, the crucifixion, the resurrection, and the ascension. The colours are predominantly red, blue, and green on a gold background.

Between St Luke's and St Saviour's Chapels, on the south wall of the ambulatory, is a very early effigy of a bishop, believed to be that of Losinga.

St Saviour's Chapel, at the extreme east end, contains more fine painting. The retable here was made in 1958 by framing a series of panels from St Michael-at-Plea church near by. Although they do not belong together, the panels, which date from about 1430–50, combine effectively. There are also some separate panels of about 1380, here again from St Michael-at-Plea. Work of this quality put Norwich right into the forefront of North European painting in the years around 1400, and it is sad that so little of it survived the Reformation.

The Jesus Chapel contains another fine painting, this time not English, the Adoration of the Magi by Martin Schwarz, 1480. A good deal of mural decoration survives, recently restored. Turning now into the north chancel aisle, one passes under the fifteenth-century reliquary arch, and then, ascending a small staircase, enters the treasury, a gift, like several others, of the Company of Goldsmiths, and opened in 1972. As well as the fine plate, it contains some excellent thirteenth-century wall painting.

Now cross back to the south side, and go out into the cloisters by the door at the east end of the south aisle. The cloister side of this doorway carries a figure of Christ over the apex between two angels, with saints each side of the angels, all under gables, a remarkable and beautiful composition. The cloisters, the largest in England, are chiefly remarkable for their nearly 400 bosses. They took from 1297 to 1430 to complete, so the carvings are very varied, and include a number of interesting iconographical schemes. From the east walk of the cloister it is possible to go to the outside of the ambulatory, where, between St Saviour's and St Luke's Chapels, is the grave of Nurse Edith Cavell.

The cloisters give an excellent view of the exterior of the steeple, the nave and the transepts. The south side of the cathedral looks astonishingly complex. From ground level upwards there are the cloister openings, the windows in the space above the cloister vault, a tier of Norman blank arcading, then the Norman gallery openings. Above them are large four-light fifteenth-century windows, the secret of the lightness of the interior, and only possible because the gallery is so tall, and finally the Norman clerestory windows. The details of the tower, with its double row of bullseyes, one blank, one open, above four tiers of arcading, and the articulation of the pilasters, can best be appreciated from here too.

Accessible from outside the cathedral to the south-west is the visitors' centre, situated above the west walk of the cloister. Here, among other things, can be seen slides of the cathedral with a taped commentary.

The Bishop's Throne

Oxford

An Anglo-Saxon nunnery founded by St Frideswide in the eighth century was turned into a foundation of secular canons in 1049, and into an Augustinian Priory by Henry I in 1111. When Cardinal Wolsey founded Cardinal College in 1525 it became the college chapel. His plan to demolish it and build a new chapel was scrapped by Henry VIII when he took over the college. In 1542 the King created the new diocese of Oxford, with its see at Osney Abbey, but in 1546 he transferred it to St Frideswide's, now Christ Church, which became, uniquely, both cathedral and college chapel. It is small by cathedral standards, even smaller than it was in monastic days owing to Wolsey's curtailment of the nave to build the south range of Tom Quad. Most of it dates from the late twelfth and early thirteenth centuries, with memorable additions later in the Middle Ages, and a fair amount of Victoriana, chiefly by Scott and Burne-Jones.

The exterior is difficult to appreciate, since for the most part it is surrounded by property not open to visitors. What can be seen from Tom Quad, however, includes the steeple. The tower was built around 1200 with lancets and plate tracery, and the spire was completed by about 1220–30. It is not very imposing, fairly short and relatively plain, but it is one of the earliest stone spires in England and the oldest of its type. Its descendants can be seen all over this part of the country.

The entrance, from Tom Quad, is very much college chapel rather than cathedral in style, and is by Bodley, 1872–3.

The west bay of the nave is by Scott; the remainder is late twelfth or early thirteenth century. The whole building, indeed, shows the point of transition from Norman to Gothic, but it is probably later than the pure Gothic of Wells and Ripon. Its scale is so modest that the architecture can be taken in in a single sweep. The elevation throughout is

The Chancel with its pendant vault

strange. The piers carry round arches, but the triforium, instead of being above them, is contained within the arches, while lower arches spring awkwardly from the sides of the piers to form a sub-arcade below. It is a system found occasionally elsewhere – at Romsey, Dunstable, and Jedburgh, for example, the last two also being Augustinian priories.

The capitals show the movement towards Gothic. Some have big, fleshy waterleaves, but more often there are leaf crockets, prototypes of the glories of stiff-leaf to come. The nave is the latest part of the building, and has the alternately round and octagonal piers popularized by Canterbury, and pointed arches in the clerestory; other-wise the same design is maintained from the earliest work to the latest. The aisles are rib-vaulted, and the north transept is aisled on both sides, while the south transept has only one aisle because of the cloister.

The east wall of the chancel is by Scott, between 1870 and 1876. He claimed to have found traces of the rose window, but how far his work represents what was originally there is anyone's guess: the front had been altered too often to admit of any certainty. All one can say is that it fits the original work quite well, and that it does correctly represent an early example of a square east end, like Southwell and Rochester, at a time when apses were normal.

The *tour de force* of the whole building is the chancel pendant vault, which also involved the remodelling of the clerestory. It dates from about 1500, and is probably by William Orchard, who made the fan-vault in the Divinity School a few years earlier, and who is buried in the cathedral. It is an extraordinary vault, a mixture of the hammerbeam construction found in contemporary timber roofs, fan-vaulting, and lierne-vaulting. The details of this highly original structure, so soon to be taken up in Henry VII's Chapel, Westminster, can be enjoyed without description. Visitors who have time will be able to see for themselves how the transition from rectangular bays to square vaulting-panels was made, how the

gravity-defying pendants work, and how the difficulty of meeting the round-headed crossing arch was resolved. It is worth remembering that it will originally have been painted.

Before proceeding to the additional chapels attached to the north transept, the furnishings of the rest of the cathedral can be seen. These include, from east to west, the retable by Bodley, the stalls with the Skidmore iron screens behind them by Scott, and the pavement, also by Scott. Both chancel aisles have east windows by Burne-Jones.

The crossing pulpit is early seventeenth century, with a sounding board. The organ is a Father Smith, greatly enlarged, but with a contemporary case. In the south transept, St Lucy's Chapel contains some beautiful fourteenth-century glass. The vestry attached to this transept is by Scott, and the best monuments here are to Bishop King, 1557, still purely Gothic, and Viscount Grandison, by Latham, *c* 1670.

The west window of the north aisle shows Jonah surveying Nineveh, a pictorial composition by Abraham van Linge, *c* 1630. The equivalent south aisle window is by Morris and Burne-Jones, *c* 1871, depicting faith, hope, and charity. The three best monuments in the west part of the cathedral are to Dean Aldrich, by Cheere, 1732, George Berkeley 1753, and in the north aisle James Narborough, 1707.

Two chapels were added to the north-east of the cathedral, the thirteenth-century Lady Chapel, accessible from the north chancel aisle or the north transept, and the Latin Chapel of about 1330 immediately to the north. Both are rib-vaulted. The shrine of St Frideswide, late thirteenth century, but reconstructed from fragments *c* 1890, stands at the junction of the chancel aisle and the Lady Chapel. It contains some good naturalistic foliage with small heads in the spandrels. The watching loft, fan-vaulted, and dating from about 1500, stands in the Lady Chapel. The one built to guard the shrine of St Alban is the only other now left in England. The glass in the Lady Chapel is by Morris and Burne-Jones, and there are fragments of fourteenth-century wall-paintings of censing angels.

The loft projects into the Latin Chapel, which contains the old stalls, simple, and without canopies. The east window is by Burne-Jones, 1859, before the beginning of his association with William Morris, and made by Powell. If any single window can be said to mark the beginning of the revival of the art of stained-glass making in England, then this is it, and nothing can be further from late medieval or Victorian stereotypes.

Much poor glass has been made since, right up to the present day, but the recovery of really rich colour and bold design, to be seen nowadays in the work of people like John Piper, might be said to have begun here.

There are a number of medieval tombs in the Lady Chapel, the best perhaps is Elizabeth Montacute's, 1354. The north transept contains a variety of later monuments, the most noteworthy being to Dean Goodwin, 1620, and Robert Burton, 1639, remarkably unpompous for their date, and the Duke of Beaufort, 1713, less modest.

St Fridewide's shrine

Peterborough

The Benedictine monastery of Peterborough was founded about 650 by Paeda, King of Mercia. In 1541 it became one of those fortunate few abbey churches to be made the cathedral of a new diocese.

Externally it is unimpressive, long, low, and sprawling, exhibiting most of the vices and few of the virtues of English medieval architecture. Its crossing tower 143ft high, scarcely a climax, though it has to be remembered that it once carried a wooden octagon, and might well, in this district, have borne a tall stone spire were it not for worries about its stability. But how different is all this from the compact, tautly articulated cathedrals of the Ile de France and the Rhineland, or even, say Gloucester. And yet, in the flat, featureless landscape of the Nene Valley, it nevertheless manages to dominate the rapidly growing city in which it stands.

The usual approach is from the market place to the west, by way of the Outer Gate, late twelfth century, but altered in the fourteenth.

From here one can pause and examine the majestic west front, unquestionably the most striking feature of the exterior. The standard authorities vary in their assessment from lavish praise to severe criticism. On the whole the praise comes from those who enjoy the drama of the overall effect; the blame comes from those who worry over the way it is achieved.

What has happened is this: Peterborough, like Lincoln and Ely, ends in a west transept. This was planned to carry two towers, but unfortunately only the northern one was completed, about 1200, and it has lost the spire, or at least the cap, which would originally have crowned it. The southern tower does not appear above the parapet at all. Then, almost immediately, work began on a great screen porch, flanked by turrets, and entered through three huge arches. For some unknown reason the original plan, to make the central opening wider than the other two was altered so as to make it narrower, which gives a rather cramped effect to a design which came close to surpassing nobility. Moreover, the north and south

91

doorways into the west transept are, as a result, out of alignment with the arches. The flanking towers of the porch have fourteenth-century spires of differing designs, pretty, but parochial, and undoubtedly frillier and less substantial than the ones originally intended. Then, late in the fourteenth century a small two-storeyed porch was inserted into the lower part of the central archway. It is pretty enough in itself, and has a pleasant star vault on the ground floor, but it further diminishes the central arch by comparison with its neighbours. Finally, the soaring verticality of the great arches, the most impressive feature of the front, is contradicted by the strong horizontal string course immediately above, and uncountered by the weak verticals of the steeples. Had the original design been carried out in its entirety, with four towers, sturdily spired, the west front of Peterborough would have been one of the marvels of English Gothic.

Behind this facade, completed in all essentials by 1238, lies the most completely Norman of all English cathedrals except Durham. Perhaps so much survived because it was later and more sophisticated than the fortress-like work of the late eleventh century, for the Saxon minster survived until the unusually late date of 1116, and even then it was not torn down as a matter of policy, but destroyed by fire.

As building began, as always, at the east end, the impressive nave comes at the end of the sequence, and was not completed until about 1175. This means it was finished about the time that the Gothic choirs of Canterbury and Wells were begun, but, until the west transept was reached in the 1190s, there is nothing remotely Gothic about the work here. It is a very uniform design, all the bays virtually identical, with no alternation of piers, a tall gallery, and clerestory of stepped triplets. The horizontal emphasis is therefore strong, but the design is held together as usual by mast-like shafts at each bay. These are not vaulting shafts, and there is no evidence of any intention to vault.

Instead, the nave boasts a much rarer survival, a painted ceiling dating from the early thirteenth century. The paintings are enclosed, vignette-like, within the lozenges that form the main design; apart from the usual saints and kings, they include such subjects as an architect with his square and dividers, and a monster greedily devouring someone. The first may relate to the idea of God the father as architect of the universe, while the latter may represent Judas being swallowed by the jaws of hell. On the west wall hangs the late sixteenth-century painting of Old Scarlett, a former verger.

The crossing tower was probably showing signs of instability in the fourteenth century, for it was taken down and replaced by a lower, lighter one with a wooden lierne vault inside. The east and west arches were altered at the same time, and the whole structure was carefully rebuilt by J L Pearson in the 1880s. The lectern is a late fifteenth-century East Anglian brass eagle.

The transepts were completed about 1130, and carry wooden ceilings similar to those in the nave, with lozenge patterns, but any paintings they may once have had have disappeared. They have east aisles, which, like the nave and chancel aisles, carry rib-vaults. The arcade piers are alternately round and octagonal, the oldest example of this design left in Britain, and over forty years earlier than its appearance at Canterbury. Though massive, they are slimmer than the compound piers normally favoured at this time.

The chancel, begun in 1118, still retains its apse, though in a considerably altered form; the apses at the ends of the chancel aisles have disappeared. The rib-vaults of these aisles are a very early example, produced not long after the pioneering work at Durham. The chancel itself has a fifteenth-century wooden ceiling, which has kept the canted shape of the early ceilings in the form of a deep coving constructed to look like a vault. It has some fine bosses.

The arcade supports are more wilful here than in later parts of the cathedral: compound, octagonal, round, and, uniquely, twelve-sided. Some of the gallery spandrels are pierced in a way that seems to foreshadow

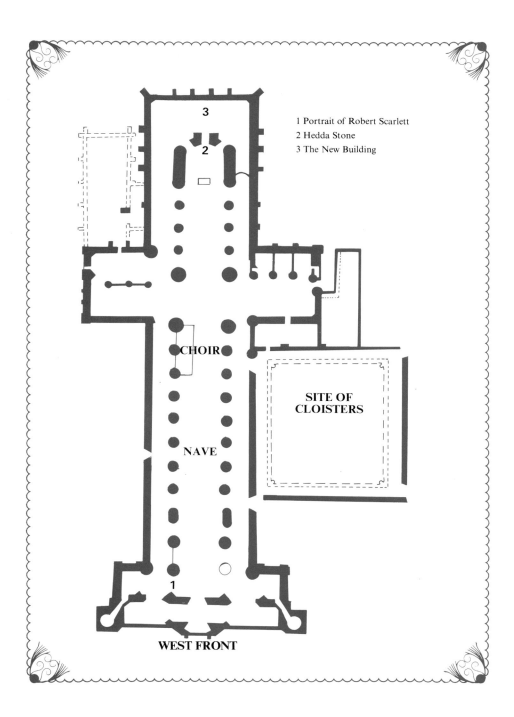

1 Portrait of Robert Scarlett
2 Hedda Stone
3 The New Building

3

2

CHOIR

**SITE OF
CLOISTERS**

NAVE

1

WEST FRONT

the plate tracery of a century later. The clerestory is of the same standard Norman design used throughout the cathedral.

In the chancel lie the Alwalton marble monuments to five of the twelfth and thirteenth-century abbots. Alwalton marble is a shelly limestone rather like Purbeck and Frosterley, but with a different fossil content. It is quarried only a few miles away from the cathedral. One of these monuments still has its early thirteenth-century tomb chest. The fine baldacchino, or altar canopy, of 1894 was probably designed by Pearson.

In spite of the survival of its apse, Peterborough has a standard English square east end. This is because of the addition of a retrochoir about 1500 by Abbot Robert Kirkton. After nearly 500 years it is still known as the New Building. Its loveliest feature is the very fine fan-vaulting – similar enough to that in King's College Chapel, Cambridge, for it to be probable that they were designed by the same man, John Wastell, who also built Bell Harry at Canterbury. The windows still have sharply pointed arches, a welcome feature at a time flatter, squarer, and less interesting shapes were usual in eastern England.

This, the most exciting piece of architecture in the cathedral, give or take the west front, contains its greatest treasure, the so-called Hedda stone – shaped like an enlarged version of a metal reliquary, with vine scrolls inhabited by animals and birds, and an arcade containing standing figures of apostles. It dates from about 800.

Outside, apart from the west front, there is not a lot to look at, except to admire the quality of the Barnack stone of which it is built. The New Building has a pierced parapet, again like King's College Chapel, and further evidence for attributing the design to Wastell.

Quite a lot of the monastic buildings survive, some in ruins, others incorporated into later structures.

Special Occasion
29 June – St Peter's Day Founders Commemoration

The North Transept

ipon

Ripon was a cathedral briefly in the seventh century; a Benedictine Abbey until the tenth century; a collegiate church until the reign of Edward VI; collegiate again from the time of James I; and a cathedral once more since 1836, the first new diocese in the Church of England since the creations of Henry VIII. Large for a collegiate church, it is quite small for a cathedral. Nevertheless it is full of interest.

The ideal way to approach is from the west so that the west front can make its proper impact. It was built about the middle of the thirteenth century, and although it sadly lost its spires in the seventeenth century, and with

them what the designer clearly regarded as his chief vertical accent, and although Scott gratuitously removed the tracery from the row of lancets above the doorways and altered the doorways themselves, it remains the best surviving west front in England before York and Beverley. The medieval diocese of York, indeed, is the grand exception to the English inability to compose west fronts, and Ripon follows Southwell in the sequence. That there is no sculpture gallery to educate the multitude may mean that medieval people would have regarded it less highly than Wells, Exeter, or Lichfield. We, with the twentieth-century liking for

uncluttered architecture, may find its simple nobility more to our taste. By comparison, the crossing tower seems inadequate. It too, had a spire, whose collapse seems to have prompted the dismantling of the western pair. As so often, then, the long, low profile was no part of the designer's intentions.

The interior of the nave was rebuilt early in the sixteenth century, probably by Christopher Scune, master mason at Durham. He left bits of the twelfth-century nave, enough to elicit the surprising fact that, like early Norman York, it was aisleless. Scune's nave has two tall storeys and no triforium. The piers, with their four shafts and four hollows between them, are a popular late medieval type, and the whole work is a well-mannered, clean-cut, light, airy design, such as people about 1500 particularly liked. It wasn't finished. Proof of that is not merely the survival of the twelfth-century work at the east and west ends, but also its survival at the crossing – where the south-west pier was renewed, but the north-west pier and the arch were not. It is a matter for amazement that the tidy-minded Scott did not remove this glaring incongruity and complete Scune's plan. The nave has a wooden lierne vault of 1868.

The south-west window has some thirteenth and fourteenth-century glass collected from various parts of the cathedral. There are two fonts, a heavy round twelfth-century one, and an octagonal late medieval one in blue marble. The early twentieth-century pulpit, with arts and crafts decoration, is by Henry Wilson. The pulpitum is late medieval, restored, and with figures of 1947. The stone pulpit which formerly surmounted it was unfortunately removed to make room for extensions to the organ, and now stands in the north transept. The fourteenth-century tomb in the south aisle has a carving of a lion and a kneeling man in a wooded setting. Traditionally the top of this tomb was used by merchants to count money when a deal was made.

The transepts date from the closing years of the twelfth century. Archbishop Roger, who began the rebuilding of the church, died in 1181, leaving the work incomplete. Its style, however, seen here and in the chancel, is very advanced for its time (about contemporary with William of Sens's work at Canterbury, and the early Gothic of Wells and Worcester). Like Worcester, the early Gothic of Ripon is not yet pure: round arches, for example, still occur. But, unlike Worcester, it belongs to the austere Cistercian tradition. The Cistercians used extremely advanced building techniques and a minimum of ornament. The pointed arch was in use for arcades as early as the 1130s in some of the Yorkshire abbeys; at Roche a scheme very like that at Ripon was used probably by about 1170, and the Ripon design could well be contemporary, though the transepts will have been built later than the choir. The elevation is worth examining carefully, as it can be seen best on the east side of the north transept. The arcade has steeply pointed, clearly Gothic arches. The gallery has four lancets in each bay, the outer two blank, the inner two open, and framed in a round-headed arch with elementary plate tracery in the spandrels. The clerestory has typical Norman stepped triplets, but the outer two have pointed arches. The flat ceiling is much later, but the aisles are rib-vaulted. Of the various monuments in the transepts the two most interesting are to Sir Edward Blackett, 1718, bewigged and looking rather uncomfortable in his semi-reclining pose, and to William Waddell, 1789, a superb piece of restrained classical elegance.

The staircase in the south transept leads to the library, formerly the Lady Chapel, famous for its collection of early printed books. It also possesses fine manuscripts, and some alabaster carvings are displayed here. The spiral staircase down to the chapter house is an untypically unfussy and functional piece by Scott. The chapter house, restored by Sir Albert Richardson in 1956, was built about 1200.

Before examing the chancel, one should visit the crypt. This must on no account be missed out, even by the most hurried of visitors, for it belongs to St Wilfrid's church

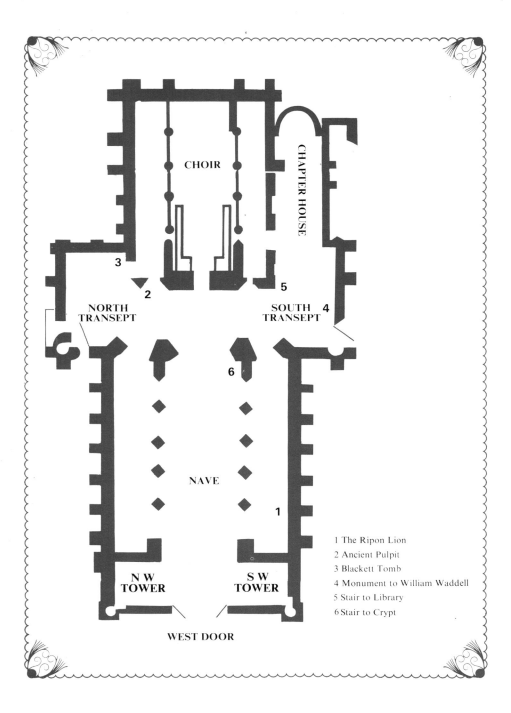

CHOIR

CHAPTER HOUSE

3

▼
2

NORTH
TRANSEPT

SOUTH
TRANSEPT

4

5

6

NAVE

1

N W
TOWER

S W
TOWER

1 The Ripon Lion
2 Ancient Pulpit
3 Blackett Tomb
4 Monument to William Waddell
5 Stair to Library
6 Stair to Crypt

WEST DOOR

97

The staircase in the south transept

of about 670. When it was first built, this
church was regarded by contemporaries as
among the finest this side of the Alps. The
crypt, though, is a simple structure: a long
tunnel-vaulted relic chamber, with passages
on three sides forming a small ambulatory for
the passage of pilgrims. Ability to crawl
through the narrow hole on the north side,
known as Wilfrid's needle, was regarded in
medieval times as a test of chastity, though
how seriously it is impossible to say. The
crypt now houses the treasury.

The west end of the chancel shows the
earliest part of Archbishop Roger's work,
similar to the slightly later work in the
transepts. The east end was extended just
before 1300 by Archbishop Romanus, with
two-layer clerestory openings like the Angel
Choir at Lincoln. The east window is a
particularly fine example of the last phase of
geometrical bar-tracery. The west bays of the

south side were altered in the fifteenth
century, when the tower seems to have given
cause for anxiety. The wooden vault is by
Scott, but the bosses are fourteenth century
and prove that something similar existed
previously.

The sedilia are a splendid example of the
icing-sugar Gothic of the east midlands
school about 1330 which gave us the choir
screens at Lincoln and Southwell, and a
good deal of fine work in other churches. The
Ripon sedilia seem to have been their most
northerly commision. Equally ornate are the
choir stalls, put in about 1490. The master
carpenter was William Brownfleet. The
misericords are excellent: a particularly
attractive one shows a pig playing the
bagpipes while two piglets dance to the music.
The canopy work is partly original in the
west parts, but most of it is by Scott. It is
similar to the stalls at Manchester.

Returning to the outside, Roger's work
is best seen in the transepts, where the
Norman element in the transition is clearer
than it is inside. The east end is a splendid
thirteenth-century composition, with a
delightful small geometrical window in the
roof space above the main east window. It is
rather like the Angel Choir at Lincoln, but
less ambitious, and perhaps rather better in
effect. The chapter house, too, can be seen
on the south side. One regrets that for
structural or financial reasons the spires have
never been replaced. If they were, the
proportions of the cathedral would be among
the best in England.

Special Occasions
2 February – Candlemas – A unique pre-
Reformation survival of the candlemas
ceremonies, including a candlelight
procession round the cathedral.
August – 1st Saturday and Sunday – On the
Saturday a procession round the city is led
by 'St Wilfrid' riding a white horse, and met
at the cathedral steps by the Mayor and the
Dean.
August – Harrogate Festival – Some major
musical events take place each year in the
cathedral.

t Albans

Not even the most fervent admirer of St Albans would rank it among the most beautiful of English cathedrals, but not even its most critical detractor could deny its great interest. Though a cathedral only since 1877, and still known locally as The Abbey, its site, the traditional place of the martyrdom of the Roman soldier to whom it is dedicated, is one of the oldest in British christianity. It became a Benedictine Abbey in 793, and a parish church after the Dissolution.

A great deal is left of the church built by the first Norman abbot, Paul of Caen, between 1077 and 1088. Not surprisingly many of its features recall the two great churches built in Caen shortly before : St Etienne and Ste Trinité ; but whereas Caen has some of the finest building stone in Europe, St Albans has none, and use was made instead of flint, and of brick from Roman Verulamium. Consequently the details are austere, even by eleventh-century standards, though originally it would have looked more impressive – plastered without, plastered and painted within, with a timber spire on its massive tower, flanking spirelets on the corner turrets, and a uniquely impressive arrangement of seven staggered apses.

Externally there has been so much alteration and restoration that it is not always easy to distinguish the early work, except for the glorious crossing tower, its Roman brick glowing red in the sunshine. It is an extremely long church, second only to Winchester among medieval churches in the whole of Europe, 550ft from west front to east wall.

Entry is by the west front or the south transept ; the latter is the ideal choice, for one is at once in the heart of the building Paul of Caen knew. The crossing arches still carry

their restored but original painted decoration, and nowhere else in Britain has so much of an early decorative scheme survived. The piers have no capitals, just plain square imposts, and both piers and arches are simply stepped, not moulded, shafted, or even chamfered. The triforium passages in the transepts look very Saxon with their lathe-turned baluster shafts. It is often claimed, without a shred of evidence, that these were reused from the previous building. If so, it was a most uncharacteristic piece of Norman respect, hardly credible in an abbot who described his Saxon predecessors as 'rudes et idiotas'. On the other hand, Robert, his architect, will inevitably have employed Saxon craftsmen to carry out his own distinctly un-Saxon design, and these shafts, ironically providing the one touch of refinement in the execution of the work, are a perfectly understandable result. If the windows at the north and south ends of the transepts look odd, that is because they are the work of that strange Victorian amateur architect Lord Grimthorpe. The south window is a composition of tall slender lancets of north of England proportions; the north window is known as the banker's window, since the proportions of its many circles echo the proportions of some of the coins of the realm then current.

From here, one can enter the nave via one of the aisles. The east bays on the north side are still eleventh-century work, with original paintings on the soffits of the arches, and an exceptionally interesting series of thirteenth-century crucifixion paintings on the west faces of the piers. St Albans was one of the largest Benedictine abbeys in Britain, and these paintings are a reminder of the need for large numbers of altars to provide for their canonical obligations. The differences in the interpretation of the crucifixion by the different painters is interesting.

Early in the thirteenth century, Abbot John de Cella set about lengthening the already long nave a further four bays to meet his uncompleted west front, a rather strange action, possibly prompted by the need to provide for large numbers of pilgrims outside the monks' choir, which stretched for several bays west of the crossing; but perhaps he was doing no more than trying to keep up with such places as Ely, Winchester, and Norwich, whose naves were already enormously long. Cella's work was in a very up-to-date early Gothic which made no attempt to harmonize with the existing bays (which may have been scheduled to come down). Stone was now imported, and the new work has a fresh beauty in contrast to the old. The south side of the Norman nave fell in 1323, and was replaced by Henry Wye in a style which blends carefully with the early thirteenth-century work, though its details are different – ballflower instead of dogtooth, for example – and it is predictably richer.

The rood screen is an early piece in the Perpendicular style of about 1350, and leads to the choir, still in the structural nave. The stalls and the organ case are Edwardian, by J Oldrid Scott, with a central section to the organ case added by Cecil Brown, 1962.

The reredos in the presbytery is late fifteenth century, but with its Victorian figures it takes a bit of believing. The ceilings in this part of the church are interesting. The choir has fifteenth-century painted panels, the crossing tower painted panels again, this time of the early sixteenth century, and the presbytery a thirteenth-century wooden vault. The apses were destroyed in the course of the standard thirteenth-century length-ening of the chancel, but the wooden vault is probably once again a sign of shortage of money.

Behind the reredos stands what is left of the fourteenth-century Purbeck shrine of St Alban, patiently pieced together from the 2,000 fragments discovered in 1872 when a post-Reformation cross-wall was demol-ished. Near by stands the watching loft, made of wood about 1400, so that the shrine and its visitors could be kept under surveillance. It is a rare survival. Its outward appearance is rather like a rood screen with an unusually large loft and parapet.

In this part of the cathedral are three fine chantries. To the south of the shrine lies Duke Humphrey of Gloucester, 1447. His

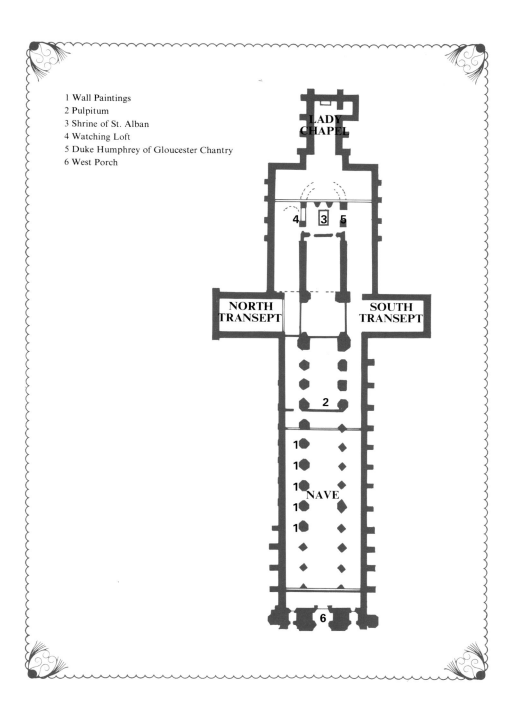

1 Wall Paintings
2 Pulpitum
3 Shrine of St. Alban
4 Watching Loft
5 Duke Humphrey of Gloucester Chantry
6 West Porch

LADY CHAPEL

4 3 5

NORTH TRANSEPT

SOUTH TRANSEPT

2

1
1
1
NAVE
1
1

6

Duke Humphrey of Gloucester's Chapel

chapel is delicately carved, but its chief glory is the reused thirteenth-century iron grille on the south side. To the north of the shrine are Abbot Wheathampstead's, 1465, not at all showy, and now containing the splendid Flemish brass to Abbot de la Mare, 1396; and Abbot Ramryge's, 1521, elaborate, and fan-vaulted, with pendants.

The Lady Chapel was added in the fourteenth century, richly detailed by Home Counties standards, but with nothing of the extreme elaboration and panache found in the East Midlands at this time.

Now let us return to the rather disappointing exterior. At the Reformation nearly all the conventual buildings were destroyed, and a grammar school was set up in the Lady Chapel. The rest of the church became parochial, but, being far too costly for its parishioners to maintain adequately, it fell into serious disrepair. On the death of Sir Gilbert Scott, the direction of restoration work fell into the hands of Lord Grimthorpe, an amateur architect with a strong personality, decided views, and a great deal of

money. St Albans did not choose him: he chose St Albans. With the huge structure lapsing daily towards irremediable ruin, it would have been folly to have rejected an architect who was prepared to bear most of the cost himself. The price to be paid was that his idiosyncrasies and prejudices were given full rein. He detested the Perpendicular style, and eliminated all traces of it in the fenestration. He added a good deal of miscellaneous pepper-pottery, particularly at the east end, and, above all, he designed the west front which the medieval abbots had never really got round to completing. Grimthorpe's work has found few admirers, even in the current resurgence of appreciation of the Victorians. Tastes may yet change, but even if at present we may deplore his self-confident insensitivity, we have to remember that but for his enthusiasm and generosity, the probability is that what we should have today would not be a living cathedral, but yet another ruined abbey. He can be seen, disguised as St Matthew, and complete with wings, in sculpture in his west porch.

t David's

St David's hides in a hollow, a position doubtless originally selected for its shelter against both weather and enemies, and without any thought of architectural effects, for it was founded by St David as early as the sixth century. Nevertheless, the valley site does mean that one's first view of the cathedral and its huge, ruined bishop's palace, is both dramatic and sudden.

The present cathedral was begun in the episcopate of Peter de Leia about 1180, and work of various dates can be traced up to the Reformation. It fell into very poor repair in the eighteenth and nineteenth centuries, and was virtually rescued from ruin by Sir Gilbert Scott. Naturally, however, his restoration has left its distinctive traces. Moreover it is not a particularly attractive building from outside. The tower is only 125ft high, but the flat roof of the nave in particular makes it seem a little overpowering in its gaunt massiveness. It is unbuttressed, and the work of three periods, the early thirteenth century for the bottom stage, the middle stage about a century later, and the top completed about 1522.

The west front is largely a reconstruction by Scott from drawings of the medieval work, replacing one by Nash.

The lower part, with the Norman doorway, is original.

Inside, the arcade is round-arched on piers with alternately round and octagonal cores and with small, sliced-off multi-scalloped capitals once described as like pollarded willows. The upper storey is fascinating. Triforium and clerestory are contained in large single round-headed arches rich in zig-zag, with scalloped capitals: so far completely old-fashioned. But turning the two storeys into a single visual feature was rather avant-garde even in the nave of York in the 1290s. Moreover, the conservatism of the Norman work is clearly a matter of choice, not ignorance, for the triforium arches are pointed, paired, and framed by a continuous roll-moulding which makes them almost identical to the eastern parts of Wells. The south windows, with their flowing tracery, were put in by Bishop Gower about 1330.

The nave roof, of Irish oak, with its big pendant bosses, is a fine piece of carpentry dating from the end of the fifteenth century. Basically it is a tie-beam construction, and it is a good example of the golden age of Welsh carpentry nowadays mostly represented by parish church screens.

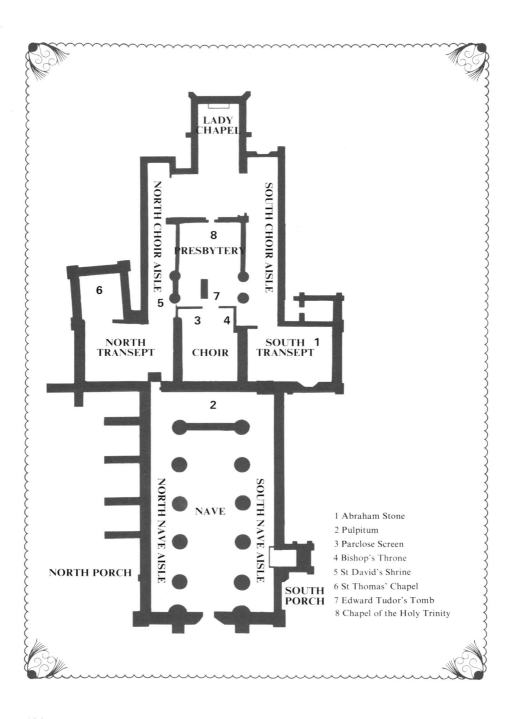

LADY CHAPEL

NORTH CHOIR AISLE

SOUTH CHOIR AISLE

8
PRESBYTERY

6

5

7

3 **4**

NORTH
TRANSEPT

CHOIR

SOUTH **1**
TRANSEPT

2

NORTH NAVE AISLE

SOUTH NAVE AISLE

NAVE

NORTH PORCH

SOUTH
PORCH

1 Abraham Stone
2 Pulpitum
3 Parclose Screen
4 Bishop's Throne
5 St David's Shrine
6 St Thomas' Chapel
7 Edward Tudor's Tomb
8 Chapel of the Holy Trinity

The tomb of Bishop Morgan is an interesting example of an early Elizabethan monument. The sculptures of the Resurrection and the apostles show a movement away from the violent Protestantism of less than 20 years before.

In the south transept are some of the ancient incised crosses which were a feature of Celtic christianity. They are of varying dates, and the finest, the cross of the sons of Bishop Abraham – clerical celibacy came late to Celtic-speaking areas – dates from the late eleventh century. The Bishop, like his sons, was killed by Norsemen.

The rood screen is a lovely piece of work of the time of Bishop Gower, whose tomb occupies the southern section of it. Its central passage has a vault with flying ribs, strongly suggesting a connection with Bristol where such ribs are a feature of the vestibule to the Berkeley Chapel. The choir still occupies the crossing, its normal medieval place, now generally abandoned for a position further east. The stalls, with their misericords, were made about the same time as the nave ceiling. Unusually, there is a screen to the east, dividing the choir from the presbytery, put in by Bishop Gower, who also installed the bishop's throne.

On the north side of the presbytery stands the late thirteenth-century shrine of St David. To its west, backing on to the choir screen, is the very similar shrine of St Caradoc; a chapel of St Thomas of Canterbury was built on to the east side of the north transept at about the same time. It was enlarged by Gower who built the chapter house and treasury over it.

The remodelled two-storey presbytery has pointed arches with rather unusual ornaments in which the ghost of the zig-zag can be discerned. The tiebeams divide the later roof into sections of painted panelling. The tomb in the centre of the presbytery is of Edmund Tudor, father of Henry VII. It has a florid Latin inscription.

Late in the thirteenth century, the chancel aisles were extended eastwards, and a roofless ambulatory was built to connect them with the Lady Chapel. It was covered in

The Lady Chapel

by Bishop Vaughan early in the sixteenth century, making the Holy Trinity Chapel, with its fine fan-vaulting, out of the western part of it. This involved blocking the lower tier of lancets in the presbytery east wall, and they are now filled with Salviati mosaics. The upper tier were replaced by a single large window, but Scott restored the original arrangement. The reredos of the Holy Trinity Chapel is a mixed grill of fourteenth and fifteenth-century carvings nicely put together. In the west wall, behind the high altar, is a twelfth-century recess containing some crosses probably from the cathedral before de Leia's, and a modern casket containing relics of St David found during the nineteenth century.

The Lady Chapel was built about 1320, but was remodelled by Vaughan in the early sixteenth century. The lead was stripped from the roof during the Civil War and the vault later collapsed. It was restored in 1900.

Special Occasions
1 March – Patronal festival of St David.
June – Onwards throughout the summer – Organ recitals by leading organists every Tuesday evening.
July – Fishguard Musical Festival – Major concerts in cathedral.

St Paul's

The diocese of London was founded in 604. By the end of the Middle Ages the Cathedral was the longest in Europe (585ft), and one of the largest in christendom. Yet if any English medieval cathedral had to disappear, St Paul's was the one that could most easily have been spared, for it had fallen on evil days long before the great fire of 1666. The spire had fallen in the sixteenth century; the nave was so shaky that it had been entirely recased in the Renaissance style by Inigo Jones, and further drastic reconstruction was considered necessary, including the replacement of the crossing tower by a dome designed by Wren. Its medieval past had been further compromised by Jones, who had built a magnificent giant portico outside the west front (giving the Cathedral a total length of 644ft). Although this cannot have suited the building which lay behind it, it is the one really sad loss.

Had the Cathedral survived the fire, it would have become an incongruous mixture of styles which the nineteenth century could not have resisted tidying up, and what we should have today would probably have been a vast and miserable hotchpotch with a strong Victorian accent. Instead, we have Sir Christopher Wren's magnificent building.

Contrary to general belief, the fire did not destroy Old St Paul's, but it severely damaged the already tottering structure. The east end was demolished in 1668, but the nave remained in use till 1673. In that year, Wren made the finest of his numerous designs for a new building in the form of an equal-armed cross. Sadly, it was too advanced for his clients, and he had to substitute an inferior, longitudinal design, based on the plan of Gothic cathedrals. A saving clause was inserted, however, which, interpreted with as much licence as he could get away with, enabled him to improve the design enormously as he went along. The foundation stone was laid in 1675, and the building was complete by 1711.

St Paul's should be approached from the west up Ludgate Hill. The west front has an imposing two-storeyed portico with paired Corinthian columns, flanked by twin

baroque towers. It is a splendid composition.

The walls of the rest of the exterior are tricked out with all the fashionable details of the day – Corinthian pilasters, friezes, rustication, triangular pediments, all of the highest quality, and at the top a balustrade (not desired by Wren, who would have preferred a plain parapet).

The exterior is, of course, dominated by the great dome – itself very simple, but surmounted by a small baroque lantern terminated by a ball, with a cross at the very top, 366ft high.

Inside, the beautiful dove-grey Portland stone brings a quality of coolness even on the sultriest of London days. The whole cathedral has a two-storeyed elevation with a balcony at the base of the clerestory. The arcades are superlatively designed. Tall fluted Corinthian pilasters rise on the inside of each pier, and a pair of lower pilasters flanks the east and west sides. The arches, round of course, are carefully detailed, and the upper storey is a study in grey stone and white plaster infilling, with transverse arches at each bay, three-dimensional arches curving in from the clerestory windows, and saucer domes in the centre. The aisles are also domed, but the oval chapels just east of the towers at the west end are sumptuously groin-vaulted. In the south-west tower is the geometrical staircase, an ingenious open circular stair with wrought-iron balustrading by Tijou, which leads to the library. It is not open to the public.

The finest piece of furnishing in this part of the Cathedral is the wooden screen to the north-west Chapel of St Dunstan. It has Corinthian columns and was carved by Maine in 1698. In the south aisle is Holman Hunt's painting *Light of the World*, a copy made by the artist in 1900 of the one he did nearly half a century earlier for Keble College, Oxford.

For those who like viewing memorials, St Paul's is second only to Westminster Abbey as a place of pilgrimage. It was not until the Napoleonic Wars that St Paul's became a popular place of sepulture for the great, and although some of the sculpture is

good, by such acknowledged masters as Flaxman, Westmacott, and Chantrey, a great deal of it is distinguished chiefly for its size. In the nave, pride of place must be given to Stevens' memorial to the Duke of Wellington, the product of 20 years work from 1857. It is an excellent example of the classical face of Victorianism, decidedly grandiloquent.

The crossing contains the four statues that started the fashion : Sir Joshua Reynolds by Flaxman ; John Howard, Samuel Johnson, and Sir William Jones by Bacon. But these are scarcely the most important things to notice, for here one can look up into the dome from the huge octagonal central space. Seen from inside it is just as impressive as it is outside, though actually, of course, it is not the same dome, and between the inner and the outer dome there rises a brick cone which supports the lantern, This can be seen through the hole at the top of the inner dome. The monochrome murals were painted between 1716 and 1719 by Sir John Thornhill, and they can best be seen from the Whispering Gallery which is immediately below. In the spandrels of the supporting arches are the first of the mosaics, which will be considered later.

The transepts are full of military memorials, amongst which Flaxman's Nelson is distinguished for the high quality of the sculpture. Here, too, is a beautiful doorcase with Grinling Gibbons carving, made from parts of the choir furniture. In the north transept is the font, made by Francis Bird in 1727.

The chancel is magnificent, though it no longer looks at all as Wren intended. Some of the alterations are for the better, others are regrettable. Architecturally it continues the same scheme as the nave. The stalls and organ case are by Grinling Gibbons, arguably the finest woodcarver Britain has ever produced. The organ, a Father Smith (Schmidt) of 1694, originally stood over the return stalls, that is the stalls which ran across the west end of the chancel, screening it off like a medieval pulpitum, but it is now split between the north and south sides. The stalls are as

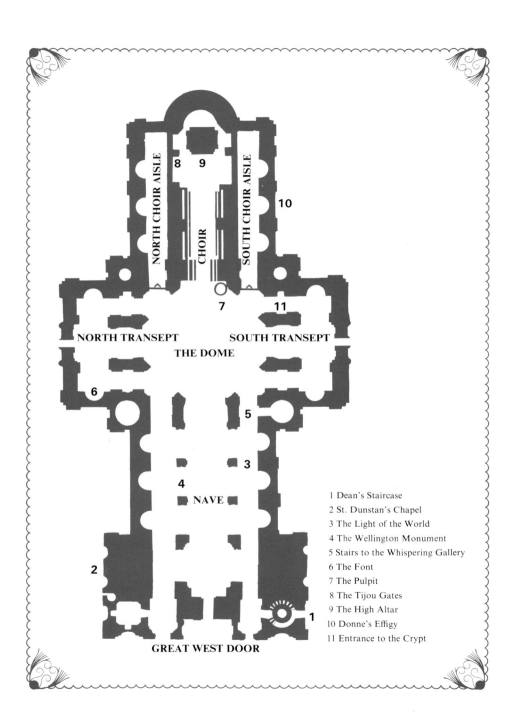

NORTH CHOIR AISLE

8 9

CHOIR

SOUTH CHOIR AISLE

10

7 11

NORTH TRANSEPT   SOUTH TRANSEPT

THE DOME

6

5

3

4

NAVE

2

1

GREAT WEST DOOR

1 Dean's Staircase
2 St. Dunstan's Chapel
3 The Light of the World
4 The Wellington Monument
5 Stairs to the Whispering Gallery
6 The Font
7 The Pulpit
8 The Tijou Gates
9 The High Altar
10 Donne's Effigy
11 Entrance to the Crypt

beautifully carved at the back as the front, with Corinthian columns, wreaths and garlands of flowers, cherubs' heads, cupolas, and much else besides.

The pulpit, though actually in the crossing, belongs visually here, a piece carefully and beautifully designed by Lord Mottistone in 1964 to blend with Gibbons' work. The fine eagle lectern opposite is by Sutton, *c* 1720. Further east, the baldacchino over the high altar is another modern piece in the baroque style, this time by Dykes Bower and Allen.

The screens at the entrance to the chancel aisles are magnificent ironwork by Tijou; his original gates to the chancel, together with his sanctuary screens are now in the east bays of the chancel arcades. The date 1890 on them represents the time of their adaptation to their present use. The original wrought-iron communion rails now form the low boundary at the west end of the chancel. Whether all this resiting of Wren's furnishings improves the chancel is open to doubt. The Cathedral is now open from east to west, and the long vista which doubtless prompted the alterations, is, as always, disappointing, destroying all sense of seclusion. The one gain is that choir services can be joined in by a congregation seated in the nave.

The monument to notice here is to John Donne, 1631, by Nicholas Stone. It has all the quality one expects from this sculptor, but shows the great Dean standing upright in his shroud, an arrangement which he actually posed for, and as disagreeable an idea as he probably intended it to be. Unfortunately, it sparked off something of a fashion.

The mosaics by Sir William Richmond, which fill the upper parts of the chancel, are part of the alterations of the 1890s, and by far the most successful part. One moves from the grand austerity of the nave to the dancing shimmer and glitter of the choir. The individual compositions are beautifully designed, and, without copying Byzantine mosaics, give a Byzantine sense of awe and mystery, which the cathedral otherwise lacks.

The extreme east end has three chapels; on the north side is the Modern Martyrs Chapel, on the south the Lady Chapel, and in the apse the former Jesus Chapel, since 1958 the American Memorial Chapel.

The crypt, accessible from the south transept, runs beneath the whole cathedral. At the crossing, under the dome, are eight Tuscan columns in a circle. Otherwise it is extremely massive and simple, with groined vaults. It contains an interesting modern nativity group, and the marble pulpit of 1860. Otherwise it is full of monuments. The finest is Nelson's under the dome. His superb black marble sarcophagus was commissioned by Cardinal Wolsey for himself, confiscated by Henry VIII, and then unused for nearly three centuries. Wellington's impresses by its massive ugliness, as plain and uncompromising as the man himself in his later years. His funeral carriage, of 1852, at the extreme west end, is a much more attractive affair. But, most impressive of all is the simple black slab which marks the resting place of Sir Christopher Wren, and the wall tablet behind it with the famous inscription: 'Si monumentum requiris, circumspice' – if you require a monument, look around you. There is really no more to be said.

alisbury

Salisbury has an advantage over other English Gothic cathedrals in that it was built on a virgin site. The see was transferred from Sherborne to Sarum about 1075, under the same decree of William I that moved Dorchester to Lincoln and Selsey to Chichester. Sarum, however, proved unsatisfactory. It was an arid spot; water was short, and on the congested site castle and cathedral quarrelled constantly. The clergy decided to move out, and the foundation stone of the cathedral of New Sarum, Salisbury, was laid in 1220. Old Sarum is now deserted, and the foundations of the cathedral and scanty remnants of the castle are all that is left inside the great earthworks.

The cathedral begun in 1220 was completed in 1266. After that, only minor works were done, except for the great steeple added in the second quarter of the fourteenth century, and, of course, it is the steeple that

distinguishes Salisbury from everywhere else. At 404ft, it is the highest medieval monument left to us. There were higher spires once at Lincoln, at Old St Paul's, and at Malmesbury Abbey, but none of these is likely to have been finer than Salisbury's, which is perhaps the most beautiful in Britain. It can be seen for miles across the flat water meadows of the Avon, shining in the sunlight or silhouetted against it, and it is this that makes Salisbury the most magnetic of cathedrals. The visitor feels irresistibly drawn to it as to nowhere else except perhaps Durham.

It is also unusual in that one does not feel an immediate urge to go inside. Because of the spaciousness of the close it is easier to enjoy from outside than most, and one feels impelled to see the effect of that superb spire from as many angles as possible.

The thirteenth-century crossing tower was probably low, and part of it at least survives as the lowest storey of the existing tower. The rest was begun in 1334 under the direction of Robert Mason and Richard of Farleigh. The fourteenth-century work respects the earlier design in its general form, but has up-to-date details like ballflower ornament. The tower ends in bold pinnacles, then taller pinnacles stand inside them to

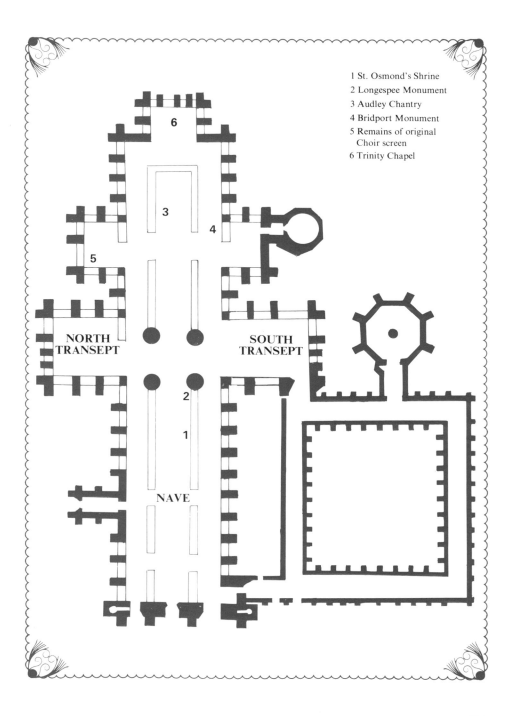

1 St. Osmond's Shrine
2 Longespee Monument
3 Audley Chantry
4 Bridport Monument
5 Remains of original
  Choir screen
6 Trinity Chapel

6

3

4

5

NORTH
TRANSEPT

SOUTH
TRANSEPT

2

1

NAVE

make the transition to the spire. The spire itself has dormer windows, then three friezes of blank tracery, but no higher spire-lights. Inside is a network of wooden struts, originally scaffolding, but left there to brace it, and at its base is a fourteenth-century treadmill used to hoist the materials used to build it. For visitors who have the time, a detailed tour of the tower lasting about an hour and a half is sometimes available.

The rest of the exterior is easily absorbed, since, a rare exception in England, it is virtually all the work of a single generation. Whether Elias of Dereham, one of the canons, or Nicholas of Ely, the master mason, was responsible for the design, or whether they should share the credit, is something scholarship has not yet resolved. Whoever it was produced a fine building, seen at its best from the north-east, where the relative heights of the various parts are most tellingly massed. The principal elements in the design are groups of lancets, very effectively varied, and strongly projecting gabled buttresses. Although it is not actually

The West Front

a very high building – only 84ft – it looks like one in spite of the spire which might be expected to dwarf it.

The west front is one of those screens so dear to thirteenth-century English architects, but which they could never quite bring off. This one was designed by Richard Mason in 1267, the last part of the original cathedral. From a distance it is successful except that the flanking turrets seem too small in proportion to the rest. Closer too the detail seems over-fussy, and all the statues are Victorian. Were it not for the odd half-arches which would be alien to nineteenth-century exactness, but which clearly did not trouble the medieval mind, one would guess this to be a Victorian front.

Finally, before going inside, it is worth noticing that no small part of the effect of the exterior is gained from the creamy-white Chilmark stone of which it is built.

Entrance is now by the cloisters in the south-west corner of the cathedral. The first impression inside is of a coolness bordering on coldness, a result of the loss of most of the medieval glass and furnishings for which the late eighteenth-century restorer Wyatt must bear most of the blame. More than any other cathedral, Salisbury would benefit from the insertion of sympathetically designed modern coloured glass. Something of the original effect can be gained from the great west window, and one or two of the aisle windows which contain miscellaneous odds and ends of medieval glass.

The architecture of the nave is elegant, and makes effective use of Purbeck. There is a minimum of ornament, which emphasizes its clean lines. The only disappointment is the squatness of the gallery openings: so low a gallery might have looked better with old-fashioned lancets, like Wells, than with the up-to-date plate tracery the architect chose instead.

There is no denying the fact that the beautiful new site so much praised by the clergy anxious to escape from Old Sarum, was marshy, and the nave piers are built on sleeper walls as a result. Wyatt chose to line up all the old monuments on these walls, with the result that they now look uncomfortably regimented. Among the best are a twelfth-century one to Bishop Joscelin, or St Osmund, it is uncertain which, that has a rhymed inscription. A slightly earlier one to Bishop Roger is of Tournai marble, and these must have come from the old cathedral. William Longespee, 1226, has the earliest remaining English military effigy. His tomb-chest is wooden. There is one outstanding post-medieval monument, that to Lord Wyndham, 1745, by Rysbrack. The clock is fourteenth century, and was originally in the free-standing bell-tower destroyed by Wyatt.

The crossing has two later alterations, strainer arches to support the piers against the thrust of the tower, and a lierne vault, both put in during the fifteenth century. The rest of the high vaults in the cathedral are all original. The main transepts have the same elegance of architecture as the nave.

In the chancel it is interesting to see the effect of the polished Purbeck marble of the shafts against the unpolished Purbeck of the cores of the piers: it is a very attractive combination. Capitals are plainly moulded, though the choir aisles have stiff-leaf bosses and there is a little dogtooth. The stalls are partly fourteenth century with misericords. The upper parts, the bishop's throne, and the pulpit are all by Scott. Among the many monuments, three can be picked out for their excellence. First, in the north chancel-aisle, is the chantry of Bishop Audley, 1524, with its fine canopy work and fan-vaulting. Secondly, in the north-east transept, there is a huge brass to Bishop Wyville, 1375, clearly showing him as the military bishop that he was. Thirdly, in the south chancel aisle, is the monument to Bishop Giles de Bridport, 1262, of stone and Purbeck, showing the earliest use of bar-tracery at Salisbury.

The eastern crossing also has strainer arches, erected late in the fourteenth century, and closer to the heavy style of Wells than to the more delicate later work further west. In the north-east transept are the remains of the original choir screen of *c* 1260, unfortunately moved here by Wyatt in 1790 in his misguided quest for vistas. In the south-east transept is a thirteenth-century cope chest and some contemporary grisaille glass.

At the extreme east end are the retrochoir and the Trinity Chapel, formerly the Lady Chapel. In the retrochoir is the splendid baroque monument to Sir Thomas Gorges, 1635, richly decorated with reliefs. Connoisseurs of this period will enjoy contrasting it with the gorgeously recoloured tomb of Sir Richard and Lady Mompesson, 1627, in the south choir aisle.

In the Trinity Chapel the slenderness of the supports is almost incredible for its period, in places just single Purbeck shafts, in others, small groups of slim detached shafts, the sort of thing that early nineteenth-century Gothic liked to do in cast iron, but unique in medieval stonework. The east window has some grisaille glass, and coloured glass of the sixteenth and seventeenth centuries.

The cloisters were a luxury. They lead nowhere except the chapter house, for Salisbury was not a monastic foundation. They were built about 1270 and use Westminster Abbey style bar-tracery. The chapter house was also based on that at Westminster Abbey, and contains a fascinating series of carvings of Old Testament scenes, basically original, but drastically recut in the 1860s.

The library contains some interesting manuscripts and early printed books, but its great treasure is one of the four remaining original copies of Magna Carta.

The close, with its wide lawns replacing the old graveyard, much the most successful aspect of Wyatt's restoration, makes a splendid foil both to the cathedral and the houses round it. The former bishop's palace, with parts dating as far apart as *c* 1220 and *c* 1740 is now part of the cathedral school. In the centre of the north range, Mompesson House, a very striking building of 1701, belongs to the National Trust and is open to the public.

Special Occasions
Salisbury, with Winchester and Chichester, takes part in the Southern Choirs Festival. Its setting rotates annually round the three cathedrals.

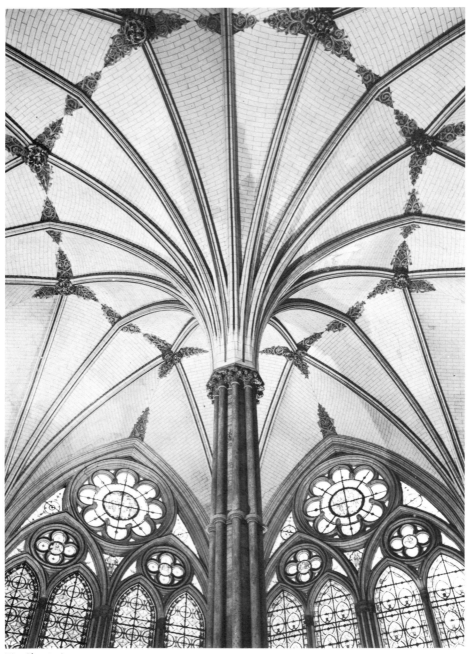

The Chapter

outhwell

Southwell was founded as an independent collegiate church, probably in the tenth century, In medieval times the three great collegiate churches of Southwell, Ripon, and Beverley functioned virtually as sub-cathedrals in the large diocese of York, and Southwell has always been regarded as the mother church of Nottinghamshire. The College was suppressed by Edward VI, but restored by Mary and confirmed by Elizabeth I in 1585. The church was raised to cathedral status in 1884.

Such important collegiate churches shared in the great rebuilding after the Norman Conquest. Work at Southwell began in 1108, and nearly everything one sees now dates then and about 1290. The western half of the church was badly damaged by fire after lightning had struck the south-west spire in 1711, but it has been fortunate in undergoing sensitive and self-effacing restorations.

The best approach is from the west. The west front came at the end of the first building programme about the middle of the twelfth century. Indeed, the blank arcading high up on the south-western tower consists entirely of pointed lancets – it is easy to see how they were derived from the round-headed intersecting arcading on the north-western tower – and is probably a little later still. It is a fine facade, and it has already been noticed (see Ripon) how the diocese of York in its

four great churches managed to achieve the essential vertical element in twin-towered west fronts which the rest of England never brought off. Southwell is the earliest of the series and perhaps inspired the others. It is refreshing to see the pyramidal caps in place, and although they were only put there in 1880, and most scholars think that Ewan Christian made them a little too steep, they are essential to the original intention. One

only has to see them to understand how much finer the west front of Ripon would be if they were replaced there.

The great west window is a fifteenth-century insertion which brings a flood of highly desirable light to the nave, and which is a fine enough composition in itself – the stepped upper transom shows an originality of design uncommon at the time – but it makes a great black gash in the Norman front, which will have had tiers of small windows beforehand. The west door is original, a rare survival, with its nice scrolly iron hinges.

Entry, however, is normally by the north porch. This is one of the earliest lateral porches in England. Other twelfth-century porches are known, but they are not common, and even more rarely are they two-storeyed, as this one is. The room above was probably where the sacristan kept guard on the church. The lower floor is tunnel-vaulted, another rarity in England.

On entry the nave appears to belong to the aqueduct type, with a gallery nearly as tall as the arcade, and a clerestory with single openings instead of the stepped triplets one comes to expect. The gallery openings are undivided, but it is clear that an unusual kind of subdivision was planned, and to see how they were intended to appear one would have to visit Romsey Abbey, Hampshire, which has a number of affinities with Southwell. The piers are cylindrical drums, short and sturdy, as are the gallery supports. There is a pleasant but restrained display of ornament, just enough to avoid monotony in what is one of the simplest Norman designs. The wagon roof was put in by Ewan Christian in 1880 and fits the architecture well. The aisles carry their original rib vaults.

The transepts are also part of the twelfth-century church. The crossing arches are splendid, with bold cable decoration on a scale rarely seen. In the north transept is a tympanum with late Saxon-style carving showing St Michael and the dragon, and David rescuing the sheep from the lion. On the east side of this transept is a late thirteenth-century chapel, now a memorial to the airmen of both world wars. The fittings were made from parts of an aircraft that crashed in France.

In the south transept can be seen the tomb of Archbishop Sandys, 1588, a high quality alabaster memorial, far less pompous and better carved than most monuments to the rich or distinguished of this period. Below the floor can be seen a fragment of tesselated pavement, possibly Roman, or more probably a later imitation made to floor the south transept of the Saxon minster.

The pulpitum is a marvellous structure of about 1330, from that East Midlands school of masons who produced the one at Lincoln and the Ripon sedilia. From Lincoln, but from the slightly earlier Easter Sepulchre there, the designer borrowed the idea of flying ribs for the vault, a conceit also to be found in the pulpitum at St Davids, and so memorably at Bristol. The east side of this screen in particular has that lushness of detail only found at this time in English architecture, which led Rickman in the early nineteenth century to christen the period 'Decorated'. There are some splendid caricatures among the tiny figures.

Admiration of the pulpitum, however, must not prevent one looking up to examine the capitals of the eastern arch of the crossing. These, like the tympanum in the transept, are eleventh century in style, and it has been suggested that they, too, came from the previous church. However it is now well-known that the Saxon style did not die out at the Conquest, and it could be that these carvings represent a conservatism based on Saxon traditions.

The chancel was rebuilt, twice the length, by Archbishop de Grey, starting in 1234. There are east transepts and a Lady Chapel at the extreme east end, a standard plan at the time. What is unusual is the way in which triforium and clerestory have been made visually one, something which had already been done at Ripon about 1175, at St Davids a little later, and was to be done at York about 1290, but which was distinctly uncommon until the late Middle Ages. The tall, narrow

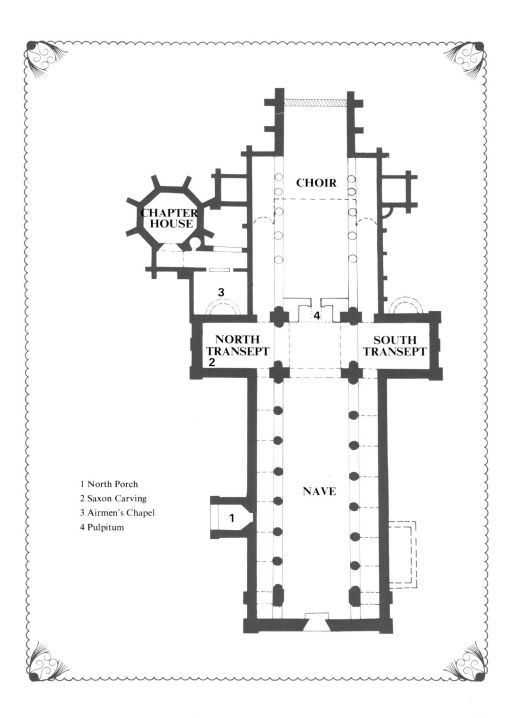

CHOIR

CHAPTER
HOUSE

3

NORTH
TRANSEPT
2

SOUTH
TRANSEPT

4

1 North Porch
2 Saxon Carving
3 Airmen's Chapel
4 Pulpitum

NAVE

1

lancets are also more typical of York and the north than of the much nearer cathedral of Lincoln. There are stiff-leaf bosses in the vault.

The brass eagle lectern and the candle-sticks were found in the fishpond at Newstead Abbey, where they had been thrown at the Dissolution. They were made about 1500. The sedilia are very similar to the pulpitum, and were probably made by the same masons at about the same time. They are unusual in having five seats. The little figures were heavily restored in 1820.

There are many fine chapter houses in England, but none is as famous as the one at Southwell. It is approached by a passage-way leading from the north chancel aisle, which terminates in a vestibule before one turns east into the chapter house itself. This complex was added about 1290, the time when stiff-leaf decoration gave way to leaves drawn from nature. Work as fine can be seen elsewhere, for example at Exeter and Wells, but nowhere is there so much of superb quality concentrated into such a small space and so easily accessible to the eye. Every capital is a joy, and the entrance arch from the vestibule has two of its orders consisting entirely of leaf carving. Purbeck marble is used for the shafts, and the net result is one of the most beautiful entrances to be found anywhere.

The chapter house itself is light owing to the clear glass in the windows. There is no centre column, and the architect boldly chose to crown his work by a beautiful lierne vault. Everywhere, in canopies, capitals, spandrels, and bosses, are leaves, with little figures and masks among them. It is an enjoyable task to try to identify the leaves, mainly buttercup, cinquefoil, hawthorn, hop, ivy, maple, oak, and vine. But although there is so much decoration it was not over-done, and there are plenty of plain surfaces to form a contrast. Not so in the 1330s, as the pulpitum here and the Ely Lady Chapel show. The window tracery uses geometrical forms, a little more adventurously than the Angel Choir at Lincoln – see the higher centre lancet, with the trefoil in its head – and

showing signs of the approach of the fourteenth century.

Outside the cathedral the unusual round clerestory windows in the nave can be seen – observant visitors may have noticed them already through the arches inside – and the south transept has a good deal of surface decoration, more interesting than beautiful. The steeply-pitched chapter house roof, dating from 1803 in its present form, is effective, and the fine buttressing of the thirteenth-century work, as against the slim pilasters of the twelfth, is worth noticing. There are a few later windows, dating from the fourteenth century (renewed flowing tracery) and the fifteenth (panel tracery).

Special Occasions
An annual list is published by the Friends of Southwell Cathedral as part of their annual report. (Present secretary's address: Easthorpe House, Southwell).

Wells

Wells was made the cathedral for Somerset in 909.

It lies in a hollow, usually an unfortunate setting, but the view from the hills near by is every bit as attractive as looking up to the brooding dominance of Lincoln or Durham. It is, indeed, one of the most visually appealing of British cathedrals, partly because of the high quality of its architecture, and partly because of the equally high quality of the Doulting stone of which it is built.

But Wells is not only lovely to look at. It is also one of the most important buildings in the history of English architecture, the first truly English Gothic building. For a century or more the work at Wells influenced most of the great buildings of the west of England and Wales, until first Bristol and then Gloucester became the trend-setters.

It is not a grand building, but one of modest and engaging charm: a feminine cathedral one might almost say, and it is set in a superb precinct, one of the completest medieval survivals in Europe. Nowhere in Britain can the medieval spirit more readily be understood than here.

What most visitors will see first is the west front across Cathedral Green or from Sadler Street. If the light is good, that cliff of gold rising from a sea of green will make him catch his breath. It is a screen front, in which the towers, though planned from the first,

are a much later addition. It is richly decorated, and forms the best gallery of medieval sculpture to be found in Britain, though some of the statues, sadly worn, are now being replaced and taken inside.

After that glorious first impression, a closer inspection is entitled to criticize details. The composition is rather crowded; there are perhaps too many triangular gables – a west country failing; the Kilkenny marble shafts (replacing worn Purbeck originals) are, like some of the statues, long and lean (Pevsner unkindly likened them to scaffolding); the statuary, based on that at Chartres and Rheims, is not as good as its models, or as other English work of French inspiration at Westminster Abbey and Lincoln; the doorways are too small; the windows in the tall blank lancets are niggly; and the towers, superb creations in themselves, do not really blend with the work below. And yet, having said all this, one returns, almost against one's better judgment to first impressions. It might not deserve to succeed, but it does. The lower parts are the work of Thomas Norris, who worked at the cathedral from 1229 to 1249; the south-west tower was added by William Wynford, who so brilliantly remodelled the Winchester nave, between about 1365 and 1395, and the north-west tower was copied from it about 1430.

It does not seem likely that Wynford intended such a blunt termination to his towers. Probably they should have had paired pinnacles at each corner. Another possibility is that spires were intended as well, an addition which would have dramatically improved the proportions. Traces of colour prove that the statues and their background niches were originally painted. Though it is difficult to imagine the effect, the likelihood is that colour would have reduced rather than increased the effect of fussiness, since it would have separated the parts visually much more strongly than natural stonework can do.

Entering by one of the west doors, the nave is seen in all its beauty. It was built by Adam Lock between 1192 and about 1230, but it largely continues the plan of the earlier chancel begun about 1176. The strainer arches at the crossing, the most eye-catching feature, were not put in until about 1340, when the new tower was causing anxiety. They are very dramatic, and whether one likes them or not, the eye probably needs something to arrest it at this point, for the nave marches as relentlessly eastwards, as the ancient basilicas of Rome or Ravenna, though the means used are completely different. At Wells, it is primarily the triforium that does it, an uninterrupted procession of lancets, with a string course above and below. Moreover, each bay of the arcade, clerestory, and vault, is identical except for tiny details denoting changes of workmen as the work proceeded westwards.

The piers are clustered, but it is worth seeing how the effect is obtained. The basic shape is an equal-armed cross, with triple shafts at each end of the arm, and triple shafts in the diagonals, twenty-four shafts altogether. The capitals have stiff-leaf in glorious variety, earlier at the east of course, and more and more lively and deeply undercut as the west front was approached. The aisles are vaulted in much the same way as the nave itself, and the windows are broad lancets which were later given tracery.

The nave contains two fine chantries, belonging to Bishop Bubwith, 1424, and Treasurer Sugar, 1489. Both are hexagonal, and Sugar's has a fan vault. From inside it there is access to a stone pulpit given by Bishop Knight about 1540. It is a very simple but excellent piece of Renaissance work, early for England, and an interesting contrast to the chantry. The lectern was given by Bishop Creighton in 1660.

The transepts are similar in general design to the nave, except that the triforium is divided into pairs of openings by vaulting shafts at each bay, but on the end walls there is no interruption, and this may have prompted the bold experiment in the nave.

The north transept contains the great clock made about 1390. Its works were renewed in 1838. The face is divided into 24 hours, with noon at the top and midnight at the bottom. An inner circle shows the minutes, while the centre dial shows the moon with its age and phases. The clock jack to the right, renewed in the seventeenth century judging by his dress, strikes the quarters with his feet, and two fifteenth-century jacks strike them on the face on the outside wall of the cathedral. The hours are struck on the bell on the crossing tower. For sheer fun, there is a turret above the inside clock face, round which knights hold a tournament as every hour strikes. The same one is struck down every time. The crucifix below, of yew wood, was made by E J Clack.

In the same transept, the memorial to Bishop Kidder, 1703, should not be missed, if only for the figure of his daughter, whose revealing dress scarcely suggests mourning. The south transept, like the north, has late medieval stone screens, but here they are embellished with fifteenth-century iron gates. There is a lovely alabaster monument, probably to Thomas Boleyn, and Bishop de Marchia's chantry, which, if it was made immediately after his death in 1302, was certainly in the height of fashion.

The chancel has been much altered since it was first built, chiefly by William Joy in connection with his new retrochoir in the second quarter of the fourteenth century. Purbeck marble was used in the shafts, and the original triforium is covered by a stone grille between arcade and clerestory. Its ogee arches may have inspired Ferrey's choir stalls of 1848, though in some ways they are more like the Ely Lady Chapel. The vault is based on Bristol's. There is no ridge-rib, the transverse arches are minimized, the diagonal ribs cross from one bay to the next, and a loose, net-like effect is produced by the liernes, almost, in its general impression, more baroque than Gothic. The east window contains its original glass representing the Tree of Jesse.

In the south chancel aisle is the Bekynton chantry of about 1450, still with much original colour, and with a cadaver below the effigy.

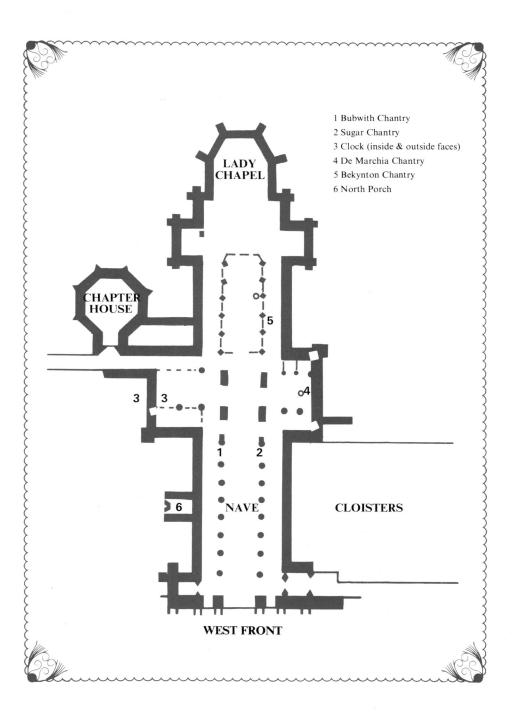

1 Bubwith Chantry
2 Sugar Chantry
3 Clock (inside & outside faces)
4 De Marchia Chantry
5 Bekynton Chantry
6 North Porch

LADY CHAPEL

CHAPTER HOUSE

NAVE

CLOISTERS

WEST FRONT

121

The retrochoir is very exciting, with its slender clustered Purbeck shafts very subtly placed to give, as a centrepiece, an openwork hexagon meeting the octagonal Lady Chapel beyond. It has a multitude of vaulting ribs, an effect borrowed, as we shall see, from the slightly earlier chapter house, and there are, indeed, rather too many, an error rectified by the delightful conceit of carving small lions to bite off the surplus ones. The Lady Chapel, perhaps by Thomas Witney, was built between 1310 and 1320, with a form of reticulation, using trefoils rather than quatrefoils in the tracery, which is unusual. The north and south windows contain a marvellous jumble of medieval glass. It is not at all apparent inside, as it is outside, that the Lady Chapel was originally free-standing, such is the skill with which Joy connected it to his retrochoir. The cope chest is medieval and still used for its original purpose.

One should now return to the north transept to visit the chapter house. To do this one ascends the famous stairs, one branch of which goes straight on to the Chain Gate, the other of which turns right to the chapter house. The staircase is late thirteenth-century work, with naturalistic leaf capitals, and a delightful corbel who holds a sweeping brush in one hand, while nonchalantly supporting the vault with the other.

The chapter house is a marvellous building of around 1300, with a central pier which supports no less than 36 vaulting ribs.

Outside, Wells has more to offer than almost any other cathedral. From the cloisters, rebuilt in the fifteenth century, or the lawn to the east of them, the crossing tower can be examined. The lowest stage belongs to the original build but it was altered about 1320, and now rises to 182ft. It is beautifully designed to emphasize verticals, with reeded clasping buttresses, groups of pinnacles on these, and two intermediate buttresses and pinnacles on each side. The bell-openings and the stage below are thus tied together, and were, indeed, originally long lancets until they were altered about 1440. The parapet is pierced with cusped triangles, a motif also found in the contemporary Lady Chapel.

Returning now to the outside of the west front, the north side can be approached. The north porch is one of the best pieces of architecture in the cathedral, as monumental as the west doorways are minuscule. There is a splendid many-shafted entrance arch, and inside there is a rib vault and two tiers of blank arcading, the lower forming a series of niches above the customary bench provided for witnesses of those parts of the marriage and baptism services that normally took place here. The upper tier of the arcading has the arch-heads interlinked in an original and beautiful way. There is a great deal of stiff-leaf carving, and the entrance doorway itself is divided by a trumeau in the centre. The surprise is that it still has Norman zig-zag, an unexpected piece of conservatism in a radical building, but similar to work at nearby Glastonbury.

Further to the north, the chapter-house staircase is a striking sight with its geometrical windows. Opposite, through the Chain Gate, can be seen Vicars' Close, which even in its restored state is the completest medieval street in England. The chapter house itself is monumental from outside, far more so than the Lady Chapel. It can now be clearly seen how the Lady Chapel started life as a free-standing octagon. Inside one tends to concentrate on the glass, outside on window tracery, and the reticulation in its unusual trefoiled form is a striking sight.

To the south of the cathedral lies the bishop's palace, moated, and dating in part from the thirteenth century. Walking along the path outside the west reach of the moat, superb views can be obtained of the cathedral towers. Turning left, through the Penniless Porch, one reaches the market square, and then, turning right into Sadler Street, the visitor is back where he started.

Special Occasions
1st Saturday in July – Diocesan Choral Festival
2nd Saturday in July – Festival of the Friends of the Cathedral
23 October – Dedication Festival
30 November – St Andrew – Patronal Festival.

inchester

Thanks to excavations in the 1960s, Winchester is the one Saxon cathedral where we have a fair idea of what the Normans replaced. It was a church of slow growth, beginning in the mid seventh century with a small cruciform building about 80ft long. Later, a detached square tower was built to the west, then, between 971 and 994 came a major reconstruction, linking the tower to the main building by a structure with side apses, which contained the shrine of St Swithun, and extending the tower laterally to form a westwork 75ft across. Finally, the east end was lengthened and given an apse, with two side-apses immediately east of the old porticus, or side-chambers. A further transeptal addition was then built further west along the old nave. Whether all these accretions were in existence at the same time seems uncertain, but the church certainly had a complex plan, and its elevation would have been complex too. Dearly though one might wish that such a Saxon cathedral had come down to us, one can understand why the Normans were unimpressed. The excavations have been covered in, and there is now nothing to be seen on site.

The new Winchester Cathedral in its present state rivals St Albans as the supreme example of the English predeliction for long, low churches: its 554ft making it the longest medieval church in Europe to survive. However, it has become every bit as much of a muddle as its Saxon predecessor. Winchester, indeed, could be said to fail every aesthetic test that could be devised by

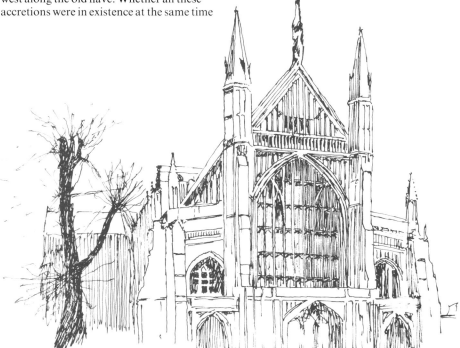

The West Front

tidy, critical minds. Nevertheless, it is an important building of great interest.

The present west front, interesting in its details, with a huge nine-light window, was built in the fourteenth century. Its general composition of horizontals and verticals – emphasized by the panelling of the walls – gives a vivid demonstration of why Rickman christened the style Perpendicular.

The interior of the nave is much more impressive, the work of William Wynford in second half of the fourteenth century. It was not a complete rebuilding, but a brilliant adaptation of the existing Norman nave. This is now by no means apparent: what must have been a three-storey elevation has been fashionably reduced to two, with the elimination of the gallery, and the substitution of a low balcony to the clerestory. The high vault is a very elaborate affair, typical of the best work of its date, and even the aisles have lierne vaults too, though of a simpler pattern.

There are some fine furnishings in the nave. The west window is filled with a medley of old glass culled from all over the cathedral. The seventeenth-century pulpit came from New College, Oxford, but the font is an early twelfth-century piece, in Tournai marble, of even finer workmanship than the Lincoln one. On the south side are the first two in Winchester's unequalled series of chantries, suitably enough, of those bishops responsible for building the nave. William of Wykeham died in 1404, one of the richest and most powerful men in England. His gabled three-bay chapel is as tall as the arcade. It has a lierne vault and a reredos inside, and a fine coloured effigy of the Bishop on his tomb chest. Edington, who died in 1366, built a more modest chantry, in which his fine alabaster effigy lies on a Purbeck tomb chest. Of the numerous monuments in the aisles – Winchester is a regrettably cluttered cathedral – the nicest are both on the south side, those to Joseph Warton, headmaster of the College, by Flaxman, 1801, and to the two Portals, 1894, where the medallions are held by an angel as voluptuously female as the most assertive in St Paul's, but prettier with it.

With the crossing and transepts we are back to the earliest days of the cathedral. The crossing was rebuilt after the fall of the tower in 1107, but the transepts are even earlier, the work of the time of Walkelin, who began building in 1079. The cathedral was consecrated, and the shrine of St Swithun transferred from the Old Minster, in 1093. The crossing piers are of tremendous size to support so modest a tower. Presumably the post-disaster builders decided to play ultra-safe.

The transepts are classic earliest Norman: three storeys of comparable height, huge compound or cylindrical piers, very simple capitals, stepped arches without mouldings, and groined vaults – the rib vaults date from rebuilding after 1107 or later still. Many of the windows are later, belonging to the time when Norman interiors were regarded as intolerably gloomy. The transepts are aisled on three sides, making provision for chapels, and the Chapel of the Holy Sepulchre, inserted between the crossing arches about 1200, has fine wall-paintings of a generation later. At one time four towers were planned, flanking the ends of each transept, but the idea was abandoned before they were built.

The library is accessible from the south transept. The main room is medieval, but has a complete set of fittings of the seventeenth century, to which many of the books belong. In the annexe are some manuscripts, including the priceless Winchester Bible, unfinished, but superb work of the third quarter of the twelfth century.

It is best next to go down into the crypt, most of which belongs to Walkelin's time. It is apsed, with groined vaults and very simple details. To the east, below the Lady Chapel, is an extension added at the end of the twelfth century.

The architect of the chancel was Thomas Witney, early in the fourteenth century. He used Purbeck piers and finely moulded arches. The upper part was remodelled 200 years later in Bishop Fox's time, and has balconies in place of a triforium like the nave, and a timber lierne vault with an abundance of bosses recently repainted.

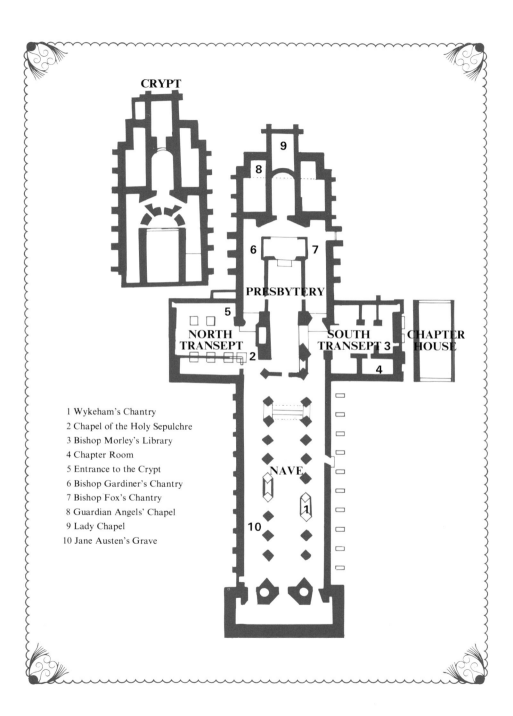

CRYPT

9

8

6   7

PRESBYTERY

5

NORTH
TRANSEPT

2

SOUTH
TRANSEPT 3

CHAPTER
HOUSE

4

1 Wykeham's Chantry
2 Chapel of the Holy Sepulchre
3 Bishop Morley's Library
4 Chapter Room
5 Entrance to the Crypt
6 Bishop Gardiner's Chantry
7 Bishop Fox's Chantry
8 Guardian Angels' Chapel
9 Lady Chapel
10 Jane Austen's Grave

NAVE

1

10

The reredos dates from the same time, though the figures are late Victorian. It can be compared with those at St Albans and Southwark. The north and south screens and the restored pulpit bearing the arms of Prior Silkstede, Fox's contemporary, are also part of the general refurbishing at this time. The stall fronts are later: seventeenth century like the communion rails and the eagle lectern. Much earlier, slightly earlier even than the architecture of the chancel, are the stalls, probably finished by about 1310, with tall ringed shafts, geometrical tracery with a good deal of cusping, and a good set of misericords. The screen to the west was designed by Scott in 1875. Earlier still is the thirteenth-century wrought-iron grille between the south chancel aisle and the transept. It is exceptionally fine, and might well be by Thomas of Leighton who designed the famous grille to Queen Eleanor's tomb in Westminster Abbey.

There are two superb chantries in the chancel, belonging to Bishops Fox and Gardener. Fox, who died in 1528, looks up at a lierne vault. Gardener was one of Mary Tudor's bishops and died in 1555. Consequently his is one of the last chantries to be erected in England. It shows a mixture of Gothic and Renaissance motifs: a fan vault, Perpendicular windows, but a triglyph frieze and delicate little shell-headed niches. Inside, somewhat incongruously, is a chair once associated with Mary Tudor.

The retrochoir belongs to the first years of the thirteenth century. Its piers are made of Purbeck marble, and the whole structure has that strange blend of coltish legginess and elegant tranquility typical of its time. The carefully restored paintings in the Guardian Angels' Chapel are outstanding, and so is a much later insertion, the memorial to Lord Portland who died in 1634. This has broken away entirely from the pompous Elizabethan and Jacobean tradition, and is a far more restrained and beautiful piece than any of its contemporaries here or elsewhere. It is attributed to Le Sueur.

The Lady Chapel belongs to the same build as the retrochoir, but it was completely

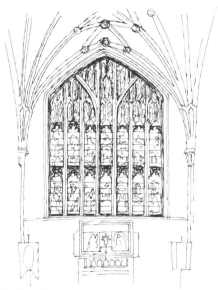

The Lady Chapel

remodelled late in the fifteenth century. Its best feature is its vault.

The exterior, as we have seen, is not memorable en masse, but some of its details are good. The blank arcading of the retro-choir is uncommonly inventive at a time when this feature was becoming boringly stereotyped in English work. Along the nave, in addition to the fourteenth-century buttresses which strengthen the Norman aisle walls, are big flying buttresses added by Sir Thomas Jackson just before the First World War. Immediately adjoining the south transept is the late eleventh-century entrance to the destroyed chapter house. Finally, in the precinct, are many vestiges of the priory buildings, mostly integrated into later structures.

Special Occasions

Holy Week – Recital by cathedral choir
June – Shipping Festival
June – Diocesan Choral Festival
July/August – Lunchtime Poetry readings
Southern Cathedrals Festival – In rotation with Salisbury and Chichester

Wynford's nave seen beyond Scott's choir screen

orcester

The see of Worcester was founded in the seventh century, and, as at Winchester, two Saxon minsters stood side by side until the late eleventh century. A Danish raid of 1041 apparently inflicted severe damage, but it was not until 1084 that Wulstan, the only Saxon bishop to keep his see after the Conquest, began to rebuild, on a Norman scale and in the Norman style.

Seen at a distance from the county cricket ground, or close at hand from the west bank of the Severn, the cathedral is a fine spectacle, dominated by what is perhaps the earliest of a group of great related crossing towers which includes Pershore, Malvern, and Gloucester. It is 196ft high and was built about 1374 by John Clyve. It originally carried a spire.

But if Worcester does not really look like a medieval cathedral from the outside that is because, like Lichfield and Chester, to all intents and purposes it is not. The Alveley

sandstone of the fourteenth-century work in particular did not wear well, and the whole cathedral had to be refaced in Victorian times. The finest of the windows, including the east lancets, the main transept north and south windows, and the great west window, are all Victorian compositions.

Inside it is a different story. Entering either by the north porch or via the cloisters from College Green, and beginning at the west end of the nave, it is worth starting by looking at that great west window, designed, like its glass, by Scott. The west bays of the nave next to it date from about 1180. The piers have something of the Wells shafting about them, but they are essentially of the Norman compound type with masts rising at each bay to form vaulting shafts. The arches are pointed, but carry simple steps and mouldings, and the triforium has pointed superarches containing round-headed stepped triplets with diagonal zig-zag rather

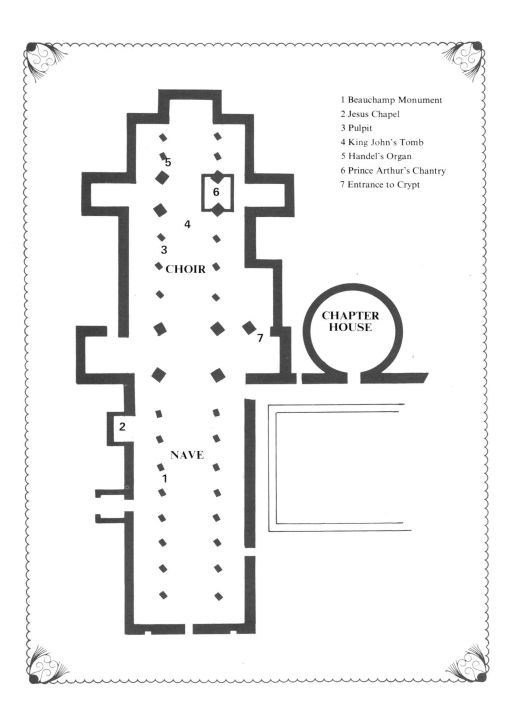

1 Beauchamp Monument
2 Jesus Chapel
3 Pulpit
4 King John's Tomb
5 Handel's Organ
6 Prince Arthur's Chantry
7 Entrance to Crypt

CHOIR

CHAPTER
HOUSE

NAVE

like the contemporary work in the Lady Chapel at Glastonbury. The clerestory also consists of stepped triple openings, the central ones round-headed, the flanking ones pointed. As an example of the transition from Romanesque to Gothic, it is interesting to compare it with contemporary work at Ripon and St Davids.

The rest of the nave was a rebuilding of the early fourteenth century by William of Shockerwick. Or was it a remodelling rather than a rebuilding? The piers stand where the Norman piers stood; they are broad in relation to their height; the vaulting shafts are suspiciously like the masts further west; and the clerestory is very like a Norman design in Gothic dress. Assume round arches on piers the same height, and consequently a taller triforium, or a gallery, starting lower, and the result would have typically early Norman proportions. The north porch contains part of an early Norman doorway, and the south wall is Norman too. Be that as it may, the capitals of the north arcade have bands of foliage rather than separate sprays from each shaft, a simplification not followed in the slightly later south side. The triforium has figures in the spandrels instead of tracery, showing William's intention to make his work conform to the earlier work further east, as will be seen later. The simple vault, added by Clyve in the last quarter of the century at a time when most high vaults were highly elaborate, shows a similar respect for the older work. The flying buttresses descending from the crossing tower were put in when it was rebuilt, a scheme also adopted at Gloucester, and less obtrusive than the strainer arches at Wells or Salisbury. The Jesus Chapel on the north side has good flowing tracery.

There are few furnishings in the nave to notice. The elaborate pulpit and the fine screen were designed by Scott, the lectern by Hardman. The best tomb is that to Sir John and Lady Beauchamp. Sir John was beheaded for treason about 1400, shortly after the deposition of Richard II whom he had supported. The effigies are fine, and Lady Beauchamp's head rests against a particularly

graceful swan. Other good monuments include those to John and Ann Moore, 1613, Bishop Blandford, 1675, Bishop Johnson, by Nollekens and Robert Adam, 1774, and Richard Jolly, 1803.

There are some early Norman fragments in the transepts, but most of what we see now belongs to the period after the fall of the tower in 1175. Much of it dates from about 1200. The north transept vault seems thirteenth century, but the lierne vault in the south transept, like some of the windows, belong to the period of the present crossing tower. There is a fine monument in the north transept to Bishop Hough, by Roubiliac, 1746. The voluptuous flow of the figures is fascinating, appearing haphazard, but in fact forming an asymmetrical balance contrasting with the simple and strictly symmetrical background.

Before looking at the choir, visitors should descend to the crypt, which belongs to Wulstan's build. It is groin-vaulted and apsed, the columns for the most part bearing simple cushion capitals, plain and dignified. It now contains an interesting permanent exhibition of the history of the cathedral.

The chancel is the finest part of the cathedral, and together with the east transepts and the Lady Chapel, one of the outstandingly beautiful compositions of English Gothic. The designer was one Alexander 'Mason', and the work, which began in 1224, was a little earlier than Master Alexander's nave at Lincoln. If, as John Harvey has suggested, these Alexanders are one and the same, and that he divided his attention between his two great works, this would explain some of the points of correspondence between them. The Worcester work contains a marvellous display of Purbeck shafts, stiff-leaf capitals, delicate many-moulded arches, and a superb triforium which develops the syncopated arcading introduced into St Hugh's choir at Lincoln at the end of the twelfth century. The openings consist of twin arches with Purbeck shafts under a containing arch with figures in the spandrels. Behind, the blank arcading consists of an even series of lancets, and the resulting counterpoint is delightful.

Most beautiful of all is the Lady Chapel, where Purbeck is used particularly richly. The ground level is decorated with trefoil-headed blank arcading with figures in the spandrels. Some are original, some are Victorian, just as they are in the triforium. The east lancets were put in by the cathedral architect, W A Perkins, about 1860. With their Hardman glass they form one of the most sympathetic and authentic-looking Victorian restorations in any cathedral. The vaults, as one would expect in the thirteenth century, are relatively simple.

Most of the furnishings in the eastern arm of the cathedral are Victorian, including the sumptuous reredos, and the stalls which incorporate a set of fourteenth-century misericords. The choir ensemble of screen, stalls, and reredos is second only to Lichfield's as an example of Scott's strongly individual high-Victorianism – at last receiving the critical reassessment and appreciation which is its due.

There are far too many monuments – a familiar complaint. The two best are the effigy of King John, made some fourteen years after his death, in about 1230, and arguably the finest Purbeck effigy in existence,

The cloisters

and Prince Arthur's chantry. Arthur, the elder son of Henry VII and Elizabeth of York, died in 1502. His chantry, still entirely Gothic in inspiration, has a beautiful screen front, an ornate reredos, and a pendant vault. Near by, in the south-east transept is a lovely little alabaster Virgin and Child still in its original coloured housing. It was made in Nottingham about 1470.

The cloisters were rebuilt in the fourteenth and fifteenth centuries, and have lierne vaults with interesting bosses. The great thing about cloister bosses, of course, is that they can be seen close to. The slype in the east range, between the cathedral and the chapter house, belongs to the eleventh century, clearly by masons working in the Saxon not the Norman tradition. The chapter house itself is early twelfth century, and unique in England in being circular, though it may have inspired the series of polygonal ones which rose later. The entrance and upper parts were altered by John Clyve. The west wall of the cloister contains what appears to be Saxon masonry.

Special Occasion
Three Choirs Festival – See Gloucester and Hereford

The Lady Chapel

ork

The see of York was founded in 627. The recent excavations necessary to strengthen the foundations have revealed much of the earlier history of the building, and have enabled a vast new undercroft to be created which houses a permanent exhibition of the Minster's history.

The architecture is fine throughout, as one would expect in an archi-episcopal see, even though none of it has the historical importance of Durham, Wells, Canterbury, or Gloucester. Almost all the glass is old, most of it dating from the fourteenth and fifteenth centuries, and although it lacks the richness of early glass, and shares the normal later medieval tendency towards rows of figures, much of it is of excellent quality.

The best views of the Minster are obtained from the city walls, especially from the south-west. The three towers are almost equal in height, which gives an unusual profile, but one wishes that the crossing tower had been completed with its pinnacles. Without them it looks too blunt against the graceful terminations of the pair at the west end.

The Minster is usually approached from the south, through winding medieval streets, or the west. The west front is without much doubt the best in England after Beverley, although it is the work of three different periods. The lowest parts of about 1300 have rows of canopied niches and bold buttressing which show that a front rather like wells but without its diffuseness was intended. In the 1330s the details changed; the gables in the arcading became nodding ogees, and the window tracery became flowing, with reticulation in the tower windows, and a marvellous composition in the great west window, the work of Ivo de Raghton, which, because of the central tracery pattern, is known as the Heart of Yorkshire. Looking at this window it is easy to see how the French 'flamboyant' style developed from the flowing curves of adventurous English fourteenth-century work. In England, flowing tracery was used alongside Perpendicular panel tracery until about the 1370s or 80s, when panel tracery on the whole prevailed, possibly because of its popularity with the glaziers, or possibly because of a

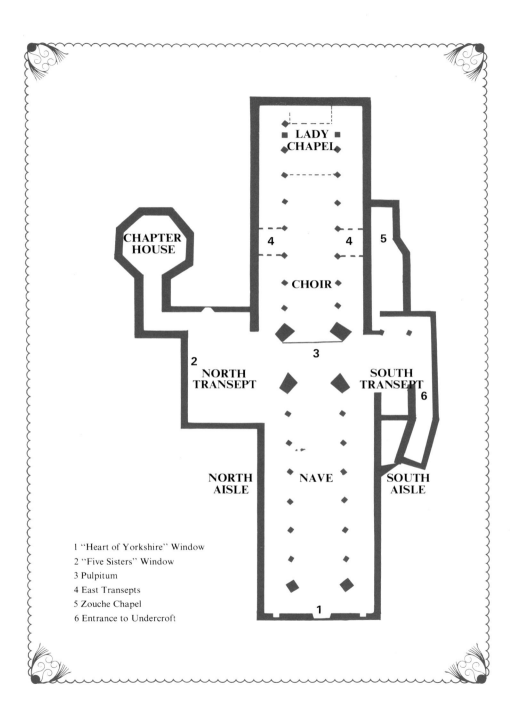

LADY
CHAPEL

CHAPTER
HOUSE

4   4   5

CHOIR

3

2   6

NORTH   SOUTH
TRANSEPT   TRANSEPT

NORTH   NAVE   SOUTH
AISLE   AISLE

1 "Heart of Yorkshire" Window
2 "Five Sisters" Window
3 Pulpitum
4 East Transepts
5 Zouche Chapel
6 Entrance to Undercroft

1

revulsion of taste against curvilinear wilfulness. This west window at York and the great east window at Gloucester are almost exactly contemporary, but they could scarcely represent more contrasting developments of bar tracery.

The southern tower was completed about 1450 and its twin about 20 years later. They are elegantly designed, with the buttresses ending just below the parapet, which is then slightly corbelled out and carries pierced battlements and eight pinnacles. The three west windows in each tower form a vivid illustration of the development of window tracery from the near geometrical work of about 1300 to the mature panel tracery of the mid fifteenth century.

On the south side the features to notice are the south porch, the rose window in the transept gable, and the enormously tall triple-transomed south window of the east transept. The flying buttresses are an early twentieth-century safety measure, added by Bodley, and it seems uncertain whether they were originally intended or not. Since the vaults, as we shall see, are wooden, they were not strictly necessary at first unless stone replacements were planned.

The east end forms a great masonry cliff, dominated by the enormous nine-light east window. On the north side, the north transept north wall contains perhaps the most beautiful lancet composition in England, the main ones, known as the Five Sisters, each 55ft tall, and above them a group of seven stepped lancets in the gable, the outer pair blank.

Entry is by the south porch, and one is immediately in the oldest part of the minster apart from the crypt. The main transepts were built between about 1230 and 1260. The piers have 'water-holding' bases, typical of this time, and the clustered shafts are alternately of Tadcaster stone and Purbeck. The aisles are rib-vaulted. The wooden high vault in the north transept was put in about 1400, but the southern one is a Victorian reconstruction by Street, the architect of the Bristol nave. These vaults are really tunnel

vaults, but this is disguised by the ribs which provide the necessary rigidity. The galleries are elaborate: four lancets to each bay; each pair under a pointed containing arch; and the whole composition united under a single round arch.

The south transept contains Archbishop Grey's monument, 1255, which makes much use of Purbeck, and has fine stiff-leaf carving. There is a trefoiled arcade surrounding the tomb chest, with a gabled roof with trefoiled blank arcading and pinnacles above. The archbishop's coffin lid was recently discovered to bear a full-length painting of him in his archiepiscopal regalia.

The north transept contains the big brass to Archbishop Greenfield, 1316, with a fine tomb chest and canopy. The most memorable windows are the Five Sisters, which contain their original grisaille glass with a small twelfth-century panel inserted, while the lancets and the rose window in the south transept have glass of the early sixteenth century.

The crossing tower forms an effective lantern. The masonry was finished in 1470, it was glazed in 1471, and in 1472 it was painted. Details of the contracts survive, including the quantities of gold leaf, and the pigments used for the decoration. The timber roof, with its bosses, recently redecorated, is original. Below, the pulpitum was given about 1500, and its gallery of kings, with the exception of Henry VI, is original.

The nave was begun in 1291, and consists of two nearly equal storeys, an arcade of 51ft, and a combined triforium and clerestory of 43ft. It was in the height of fashion when it was designed, and looks forward quite distinctly to the approach of the Perpendicular style. The timber vault was completed in 1354, but burnt in 1840 and replaced by Smirke. Most of the aisle windows contain glass of about 1310–20, and include such scenes dear to the medieval mind as St Nicholas resuscitating the pickled boys (south aisle east), St John converting the people of Ephesus from a vat of boiling oil (south aisle, third from east), the tortures of St Catherine (north aisle east), and a woman beating her husband (north aisle, third from east). The glass was well restored in the eighteenth century by W Peckitt. The contract for the great west window is dated 1338, and a little twelfth-century glass has been reset in the clerestory.

The lectern dates from 1686, and the pulpit, also seventeenth century in style, was designed by Sir Ninian Comper in 1948. To the south of the east end of the nave a library was added early in the fifteenth century. It is now the minster shop.

One should begin a tour of the east end by going down into crypt (not the undercroft, which will be left till last). The crypt is a muddled building of various dates, but a little of Thomas of Bayeux's work can be seen in the arches to the north and south turrets which originally rose between his choir and the transept apses. Much of it belongs to Archbishop Roger's time, between 1154 and 1181, including the Durham-style incised piers, one of the last times this form of decoration was to be used. The font cover is by Comper, 1946, who could design as happily in the Gothic as in the classical style.

The east end above ground was rebuilt between 1361 and about 1400, starting at the east end. Once the presbytery had reached the old choir, this was demolished and replaced. Both choir and presbytery keep the two-storey elevation of the nave, but the style is now distinctly Perpendicular, an early example for the north of England. The aisles are rib-vaulted, but the wooden high vaults are replacements by Smirke after the fire of 1829, as are the stalls, both very convincing.

Among the glass, the east window, glazed between 1405 and 1408 by John Thornton of Coventry, takes pride of place. Its theme is God as Alpha and Omega, the Beginning and the End, and the scenes are correspondingly from Genesis and Revelation. The extensive representation of the Apocalypse is said to be unique in medieval glass. Another fine window is the St William window in the north-east transept, glazed in 1422, where 100 panels show scenes from the Saint's life.

Two of the mass of monuments can be picked out for visitors who do not have time to explore them in detail. One is to Admiral Medley, 1747, by Cheere, with a represent-ation of a naval battle on the sarcophagus, rather like the later ones in the Sailors' Chapel at Chichester. This stands in the north presbytery aisle. In the south aisle opposite is the small but first class alabaster memorial to Anne Benet, 1615, by Nicholas Stone.

South of the south choir aisle are the consistory court, a vaulted vestry, and the Zouche Chapel. This chapel, built between 1342 and 1352, still uses Purbeck marble. It has a nice tierceron vault, miscellaneous glass, and two survivors of the old stalls.

The late thirteenth-century chapter house, approached from the north transept, bears many points of correspondence with the one at Southwell. It is reached by a vestibule with some stiff-leaf, but rather more naturalistic leaf carving. The windows in this passage were put in a little later, at the beginning of the fourteenth century. They fill the spaces between the buttresses and are an early example of the movement towards the 'glasshouse' ideal in vogue towards the end of the Middle Ages and beyond, which gave us such buildings as King's College Chapel, Cambridge, and of which the Gloucester presbytery is the first major example. The chapter house itself, like the one at Southwell, has no central pier, though its vault, less daringly, is made of wood, the earliest of the timber vaults in the minster. Each seat is canopied, and there is a frieze of naturalistic foliage above the canopies. The entry has a trumeau, or central dividing shaft, and above it on the inside is a contemporary but *ex situ* statue of the Virgin. A door and two cope chests exhibit scrolly thirteenth-century ironwork.

Finally the undercroft. This contains the most ambitious cathedral museum so far created. Its many fascinating exhibits cannot be described here, but two must be mentioned. The first is that section of the footing of the walls of Thomas's church which show they were plastered and painted outside with red lines to give a mock-ashlar finish, smarter than the rough ashlar which actually faced the walls. Thomas's nave walls, incidentally, have the same foundations as the piers of the present arcade, which explains the unusual width of the nave. The second is even earlier. The minster overlies the Roman legionary fortress of Eboracum, and an early fourth-century room with painted plaster has been excavated and displayed.

Special Occasions
Sunday after Epiphany – Procession with Choirs of the Minster and St Peter's School
Holy Saturday – Easter Vigil, in darkened Minster, with candlelight blessing of the font in the crypt.
28th June – Dedication/Patronal Festival
Northern Cathedrals Festival – Triennially in rotation with Ripon and Durham.

A detail from the carving on the choir screen

ppendix

All the cathedrals mentioned here are well worth seeing. Some, indeed, are almost as interesting as those previously described. Such buildings are marked with an asterisk.

Aberdeen – St Machar

Area evangelised by Machar, a follower of Columba – see founded by David I, 1136 – mostly built between 1400 and 1530 – east parts ruined by fall of crossing tower in 1688 – nave in use as parish church.

West front This is built of granite. Either side of a window of seven tall round-headed lancets stand early 15th-century machi-colated, castle-like towers with slit windows. The later spires have bold crenellated bands and tiny spire-lights.
Nave ceiling The heraldic ceiling of the nave was completed about 1520. It is of panelled oak with forty-eight shields. This, with the screen and stalls of King's College Chapel near by, constitutes the most important pre-Reformation woodwork left in Scotland.

Bangor – St Deiniol

Founded about 525 – Deiniol made bishop 546 – present cathedral built after 1290, mostly between 1470 and 1530.

Towers Bangor has two towers in axis, like Ely and, formerly, Hereford, but not a common design. The low crossing tower is the earlier, with fine fourteenth-century piers and arches inside. The sturdy early sixteenth-century western tower is also short – less than 70ft high.
Mostyn Christ A fine and rare wooden figure of Christ wearing the crown of thorns before the crucifixion, carved in 1518.

Brechin – Holy Trinity

See founded by David I *c* 1140 – bones of existing nave 13th-century, though much altered – chancel rebuilt on medieval foundations by Honeyman, 1900.

North-west tower This tower, completed in the 14th century, together with its stone spire and the satellite spirelet on the stair turret, forms one of the best medieval steeples in Scotland.
South-west tower This formerly free-standing, Irish-style round belfry was built about 990, with a later octagonal stone cap. The sculptured doorway is above ground level, emphasizing its defensive role, and the interior is divided into seven storeys accessible by ladders.

Brecon (Aberhonddu) – St John the Evangelist

Benedictine Priory founded early 12th century – became parish church at Dissolution – Cathedral of new diocese of Swansea and Brecon 1923.

Chancel The rib-vaulted 13th-century chancel has a beautiful simplicity. The windows consist of groups of stepped and shafted lancets.
Font This was made in the 11th or 12th century and has interesting, if barbaric, carving.
Cresset stone A rare example, the largest in Britain, of a once common form of lighting, an alternative to candles.

Birmingham – St Philip

Designed by Thomas Archer as a parish church, 1709 – completed 1725 – chancel extended by Chatwin, 1883 – cathedral of new diocese 1905 – all exterior stonework refaced.

Tower A bold design, with reminiscences of Wren and Borromini.
Interior The interior is plastered, and the harmony between the good 18th-century work in the nave and the equally good 19th-century work in the chancel is very enjoyable. The east and west windows are

fine examples of the work of Burne-Jones.

Bury St Edmunds (St Edmundsbury) – St James

Early 16th-century parish church, with nave probably by John Wastell – made Cathedral of a new diocese 1914 – chancel and transepts 1960 by Dykes-Bower, replacing chancel by Scott – further building planned, including crossing tower.

Main features

Bell-tower This is the richly decorated early twelfth century gateway to the abbey, and stands just to the south of the cathedral.
Chancel and transepts An incredibly conservative but very effective building in almost pure late medieval East Anglian Gothic, incorporating flint-flushwork panels outside. It blends well with the old nave.

*Carlisle – Holy Trinity, formerly St Mary

Augustinian Priory, founded by Henry I and raised by him to cathedral status 1133 – some original work, but more of 14th century – most of nave destroyed by Scots during 1640s.

Main features

Chancel The east window, 51ft high and with rich flowing tracery is a 14th-century masterpiece. It contains glass by Hardman, 1861. The arcade piers have capitals illustrating the labours of the months. A hammerbeam roof was intended, but a wagon ceiling was put in instead about 1530, though the hammerbeams were left in position. The painting of stars in a blue sky is a Victorian design.
Woodwork The stalls are early 15th century. There is an early 16th-century flamboyant screen showing Scottish influence, and Dean Salkeld's screen, of the 1540s, is a fine example of the English early Renaissance style.

*Chester – Christ and St Mary

Original church founded 10th century – Benedictine Abbey 1092 – Cathedral of a new diocese 1541 – red sandstone weathered badly – exterior now mostly 19th century –

interior of north transept *c* 1100 – rest mostly 1280–1540.

Main features

Timber ceilings There are excellent timber ceilings throughout the cathedral; that on the north transept dates from *c* 1520; the nave and chancel ones, in the form of lierne vaults, are by Scott, *c* 1870.
Choir timberwork The stalls are one of the best sets in England. They were made in the 14th century, and well restored in the 19th century. They have fine misericords, arm-rests, and popy-heads. The organ loft and case are among Scott's best designs.
Consistory court In the unfinished SW tower is the only surviving example of a bishop's consistory court room. It dates from 1636.
Bell-tower This is the most recent addition to the cathedral; it stands – detached – to the SE. Designed by George Pace, it was built in 1975 of concrete, brick, and slate.

*Chichester – Holy Trinity

See moved from Selsey 1080 – cathedral begun 1091 – consecrated 1184 – burned to a shell 1187 – rebuilding complete 1199 – further extension, alteration, and repair until the 15th century – crossing tower and spire collapsed 1861 – carefully rebuilt by Scott – NW tower collapsed in the 17th century – rebuilt by Pearson 1901.

Main features

Bell-tower Now the only detached medieval cathedral belfry left, it was built between 1375 and 1450.
Retrochoir A perfect example of the transition from Norman to Gothic. It dates from 1187–99, and should be compared with near-contemporary work at Canterbury, Oxford, Ripon, and Worcester.
Pulpitum The Bell-Arundel screen was made in the 15th century, dismantled shortly before the collapse of the steeple, and restored to its rightful position in memory of Bishop Bell in 1960.
Stone panels Two early 12th-century stone panels, probably from a choir screen, are preserved in the south choir aisle. One represents Christ at the house of Mary in

Bethany, the other the Raising of Lazarus. Though they cannot be earlier than about 1125, the emotional power of the figures recalls earlier work rather than impassive 12th-century carving, and they are among the finest things of their period to survive anywhere.

Modern furnishings These are among the most notable features of Chichester. The three most important are the Sutherland painting *Noli me tangere*, 1961; the pulpit by Geoffrey Clarke and Robert Potter, 1966; and above all, the reredos tapestry by John Piper, 1966.

Clifton – SS Peter and Paul (RC)
Designed by Percy Thomas and Partners – built 1970–73 of reinforced concrete with Aberdeen granite panels outside, for only £800,000 – centrally planned like Liverpool Metropolitan Cathedral.

Main features
Interior Concealed lighting has given strong illumination entirely without glare. The concrete work proves that this medium can actually be beautiful, a rare accomplishment, and the overall effect of great simplicity is in fact achieved by considerable technical ingenuity.
Glass The only two coloured windows, in the narthex, are by Henry Haig. They use abstract symbolism, but employ rounded forms, a departure from the angularity of the 1960s.
Stations of the Cross Sculpted in concrete by William Mitchell.
Other Sculpture Notable among the other sculpture are the font, by Simon Verity, and the bronze statue of Mary, Mother of the Lord, by Terry Jones.

Derby – All Saints
Parish church made cathedral of new diocese 1927 – tower early 16th century – rest 1723–5 by James Gibbs.

Main features
West Gallery This was added in 1732–3, and is delicately curved with Ionic columns.
Screens These are magnificent pieces of ironwork by Robert Bakewell, *c* 1750. The communion rails may also be his work.

Dunkeld – St Columba
Old see revived by Alexander I, early 12th century – present building 13th century and later – nave and tower 15th century – damaged at Reformation and virtually in ruins by 1600 – various restorations after further neglect and damage – chancel in use as parish church – rest in care of Department of the Environment.

Main features
Site The site is magnificent, with park-like grounds sloping gently down to the Tay.
Nave The gallery openings are odd, being semi-circular, like the top part of a Norman arch, subdivided by V-shaped tracery bars into two lancet heads. It is as though the bottom half of the composition is missing, but this is clearly how the design was planned. The flowing tracery of the aisle windows is attractive and inventive.

Edinburgh – St Giles
Correctly the High Kirk of Edinburgh – a cathedral only during part of 17th century – late medieval church, tidied up and recased in 1829 in curvilinear Gothic.

Main features
Crown steeple This was added about 1500, and is the most individual accent in the Old Town's famous skyline, though less fine than the one at Newcastle.
Sculpture There is some good late medieval carving, especially in the pier-bases, capitals, and vaults of the chancel and the Preston and Albany Aisles.
Thistle Chapel The Chapel of the Knights of the Thistle was added by Robert Lorimer in 1911.

Edinburgh – St Mary (Episcopal Church of Scotland)
Designed by Sir Gilbert Scott – begun 1874, completed 1917 – one of Scotland's finest Victorian buildings.

Main features
Exterior The three grand spires, the tallest 275ft high, inevitably recall Lichfield, which the building does not otherwise resemble. The west front is a beautiful composition

which Scott ranked among his best works.
Choir vault The vaulting of the easternmost
bays of the choir, giving the effect of an apse
to a square east end, is original and effective.

Elgin – Holy Trinity
See of Moray founded by Alexander I in
1107, but site of cathedral only settled at
Elgin 1224 – mostly 13th century and repair
work after fires in 1370 (accidental) and 1390
(deliberate – by the Wolf of Badenoch) – lead
stripped from roofs 1567 – Cromwell's
troops smashed west window – crossing tower
fell 1711, causing tremendous damage.

Main features
The ruination of Elgin is tragic, since there is
little doubt that it was the finest medieval
cathedral in Scotland. Enough survives to
indicate its quality.
West front The twin-towered west front is
more French than English in inspiration, and
all the better for it. The towers were, of
course, spired. The west portal is a grand
13th-century piece, subdivided by a trumeau
in the 15th century.
East gable This shows the limpid elegance of
lancet composition at its best, and once had
a rose window.
South transept The round-headed windows
above lancets, prove how late the transitional
phase from Romanesque to Gothic lasted in
Scotland.
The chapter house This is vaulted and contains
interesting carving.

Guildford – The Holy Spirit
Diocese created 1927 – cathedral designed by
Sir Edward Maufe – begun 1936, completed
1966 – crossing tower a fine landmark – apart
from Westminster, the only major cathedral
in Britain to be built almost entirely of brick.

Main features
Interior The plastered interior is light and
tranquil, Gothic reduced to essentials of
outline, and with a strong sense of aspiration
and vertical line virtually absent from
English medieval cathedrals.
Furnishings Most of the furnishings are
unworthy of the architecture, but among the

exceptions are Maufe's sanctuary carpet and
some engraved glass by John Hutton.

*Hereford – St Mary and St Ethelbert
Founded late 7th century – present church
started *c* 1110 – much 13th and 14th-century
work – west tower collapsed 1786 – much of
cathedral now by Wyatt, 1788, Cottingham
1842, and Scott, 1856 – built of local pink
sandstone.

Main features
North transept The best architecture in the
cathedral, built in the time of Bishop
Aquablanca in the mid 13th century. The
openings have early bar-tracery, and include
spherical triangles. The arches are almost
straight-sided. The tombs of Aquablanca
and Bishop Cantelupe are also excellent.
Lady Chapel A wide room with many-shafted
windows built *c* 1220–40.
Mappa Mundi A late 13th-century map of the
world displayed in the north chancel aisle.
Crossing tower This was built *c* 1310 and has
masses of ballflower decoration.

Iona – St Columba
Monastery founded by Columba 563 –
possible remains of his cell excavated –
bishopric of the Isles set up 15th century, but
without a fixed cathedral until Iona chosen
1506 – church restored from ruin after 1893 –
monastic buildings rebuilt since by Iona
Community.

Main features
Much of the church belongs to the time when
it was raised to cathedral status. Some of the
stonework is red Mull granite.
Crossing tower This has unusually large
traceried windows.
West Highland carvings Fine examples of
West Highland carving can be seen inside the
cathedral in the chancel capitals and sacristy
door, and in the museum on many of the
tombstones of the kings and nobility buried
here.
Communion table A good piece making
extensive use of the lovely green Iona
serpentine found near St Columba's Bay.
High Crosses Outside the cathedral stand the

magnificent 9th-century St Martin's Cross, a plastercast of the equally magnificent but gale-damaged St John's Cross, and part of St Matthew's Cross.

*Lichfield – St Mary and St Chad

Founded by Chad, 669 – see transferred to Chester, then Coventry – became co-cathedral with Coventry 1130 – sole cathedral on destruction of Coventry at Reformation – badly damaged in Civil War, and by neglect and decay since – now largely *c* 1220–1320 in its bones but 1857–1901 (G G and J O Scott) in its flesh.

Main features

Stone spires Known as the Ladies of the Vale, the three stone spires give Lichfield its superb silhouette. The central one has been rebuilt twice, *c* 1666 and 1795. The western ones date from *c* 1330.

Lady Chapel Built about 1310, it is unusual for its date in being unaisled. As a result it has fine, long windows, with conservative tracery, now filled with 16th-century Flemish glass. It has a polygonal end, rare in England, and inside at least, is rather like an English version of the Sainte Chapelle, Paris.

Choir screen Designed by Scott, and made by Skidmore of Coventry from iron, brass, and copper, 1863. It was restored in 1973 and now glows richly with colour. It leads to the choir stalls, tiled pavement, and reredos which give Lichfield the finest Victorian chancel fittings in Britain, rivalled only by Worcester.

The Sleeping Children A sentimental, but touching memorial by Chantrey to two small sisters, 1814.

St Chad's Gospels A magnificent early 8th-century manuscript in the Northumbrian tradition. This, the great treasure of the cathedral, is not normally on view, and can at present only be seen by prior arrangement with the Librarian.

Llandaff – St Peter and St Paul

See founded *c* 560 – mostly built *c* 1120–1280 – restorations 18th century, 19th century, and, after bomb damage, 20th century.

Main features

West front This has two towers. The north-west, or Jasper tower, was built *c* 1500, with a Gloucester crown of the Victorian restoration. The South-west, or Prichard tower, with its Normandy-type spire was built *c* 1860, replacing one destroyed in a storm in the 18th century.

Rood screen Designed by George Pace in the form of a concrete arch surmounted by the organ case which is decorated by pre-Raphaelite figures from the previous choir stalls. On the west side, facing the congregation, stands the great *Christ in Majesty* by Epstein.

Pre-Raphaelite work Two splendid pieces remain: in St Dyfrig's Chapel the porcelain panels of the six days of creation, by Burne-Jones, using Elizabeth Siddal as his model; and, in St Illtyd's Chapel, the triptych *The Seed of David*, by Rossetti.

Manchester – St Mary

Collegiate in the Middle Ages – parish church thereafter – cathedral of new diocese 1847 – a 15th-century and 19th-century building with recent repairs after war damage.

Main features

Choir stalls These date from the early 16th century and are among the best in Britain. They have superb canopies and good misericords.

Roofs There are fine original timber roofs in the nave and choir.

Tapestries In the Lady Chapel are tapestries designed by Austin Wright and made by Theo Moorman, 1957, a rare period for good furnishing.

Relief There is a relief by Eric Gill, 1933, of the Christ Child with Saints, over the entrance to the south annexe.

Newcastle – St Nicholas

Very large 14th-15th century town church – cathedral of new diocese 1882.

Main features

Crown steeple This dates from the mid 15th century and is the oldest and best in Britain, though it has been rebuilt twice, in the

17th century and the 19th century.
Font cover A very tall canopy of *c* 1500, standing on a heraldic font of Frosterley marble.
Library A Palladian library was added to the south of the church in 1736.

North Elmham, Norfolk
Extensive ruins of 10th-11th-century cathedral of East Anglia, turned into bishop's hunting lodge in the 14th century.

Main features
The church had three towers, one at the west end, and two in the re-entrant angles of the transept. The transept is uninterrupted from north to south, and the apse opens directly off it without a chancel. It must be visualised as a tall, narrow building, its height emphasized by the three steeples.

Norwich – St John the Baptist (RC)
Designed by G G Scott Junior and J O Scott – begun 1884, finished 1910 – 13th-century lancet style – one of the finest catholic churches in Britain – much use of Frosterley marble – recently raised to cathedral status for the new diocese of East Anglia.

Main feature
Glass The windows by the Powells, father and son, with their medallions and rich, jewel-like colours admirably complement the architecture.

Portsmouth – St Thomas
An amazing chapel-of-ease – parish church 1320 – cathedral 1927 – choir and transepts *c* 1180–1220 – tower and east nave 17th century – west nave 1930s, incomplete.

Main feature
Choir This is a fine piece of transitional building of the late 12th century, with an arcade of two large bays with round arches each containing two smaller pointed arches.

Rochester – Christ and St Mary
Second oldest English see – founded 604 by St Augustine – present building shows all medieval styles, but severely restored and partly rebuilt in the 19th and 20th centuries.

Main features
Main west doorway This dates from *c* 1150–75, and contains good, though worn sculpture, and an early use of purbeck marble.
13th-century woodwork Fragments of the 13th-century pulpitum and the seating of *c* 1227 are incorporated in their successors. They are the earliest survivors of their kind in England.
Monuments Two are outstanding: that of Bishop Bradfield, 1283, where the fashion for split-cusped tracery known as 'Kentish' may well have begun; and that of Lady Ann Henniker, by Banks, 1792, with superbly carved figures of *Truth* and *Time* in Coade (ie artificial) stone.

St Andrews – St Andrew
Abbey probably founded in the 8th century – bishop's seat 908 – Augustinian priory in the 12th century – metropolitan church and archbishopric 1472 – fell into ruin after Reformation.

Main features
Sarcophagus In the museum, among other interesting relics of the early church, is the superb sarcophagus made to house the relics of St Andrew.
Church of St Rule Predecessor of the present cathedral, this tiny church, though ruined, is more complete than its successor. It is probably early 12th century. Its tower is 108ft high.
East gable This dates from *c* 1160, and is unusual for its time in being straight-ended, not apsed, perhaps a sign of the strength of Celtic traditions.

St Asaph – (Llanelwy) St Asaph
Founded in the 6th century – mostly 14th-15th century – restored from near ruin by Scott 1869–75.

Main features
Choir stalls These are a good, fairly plain set, dating from the 15th century.
Library Among other things, the library contains Salusbury's Welsh New Testament of 1567, and William Morgan's Welsh Bible of 1588. It can be seen on application to the Verger.

Southwark – St Saviour and St Mary Overie

Augustinian Priory of St Mary Overie founded 1106 – parish church after Dissolution – nave rebuilt by Blomfield 1890–7 – cathedral 1905.

Main features

Retrochoir Built about 1220, this is an elegant room, of four equal naves, which is unusual, and slim, simple piers.

Chancel Also early 13th century, the chancel has one of the earliest triforia, as against galleries, in Britain. The reredos dates from 1520 with 19th-century figures. The chancel also contains the tomb of Lancelot Andrewes, 1626.

North transept This contains the interesting memorial to Lady Clarke, 1633. To the east of the transept is the Harvard Memorial Chapel, furnished in 1907, which will be of particular interest to American visitors.

Truro – St Mary

New diocese 1880 – cathedral designed by J L Pearson and completed by his son in 1910 – a scholarly pastiche mixing 13th-century English and Norman-French forms – concrete hall and chapter house by J Taylor, 1967.

Main features

South aisle This was retained from the old parish church, and was built between 1504 and 1518, a good example of late medieval Cornish vernacular.

Baptistery A beautiful example of Pearson's meticulous medievalism.

Westminster (RC)

Site bought by Cardinal Manning 1867 – cathedral designed by John Bentley in Byzantine style – built 1895–1903 – red brick with bands of stone.

Main features

Campanile This 284ft bell-tower, similar to the one at Siena, is still one of the features of the Westminster skyline in spite of modern high-rise building.

Marble decoration The marble facing of the interior, though incomplete, is unique in Britain. Marble was brought from Greece, Italy, France, and Ireland. There is also incomplete mosaic decoration. Where the work has been finished, the effect is awe-inspiring and beautiful.

Stations of the Cross Eric Gill at his best, 1913–18.

Chapel of St Andrew The stalls here, by Ernest Gimson, *c* 1912, are of magnificent quality, inlaid with ebony and ivory.

Treasuries

More and more cathedrals are now displaying their plate, and often the plate from other neighbouring churches, together with antique vestments, etc. in newly designed treasuries. Some of these are the gift of the Company of Goldsmiths. They have rarely been mentioned in the text, since this, like refreshment rooms and shops, is a rapidly expanding development, and information would soon become out of date. Among cathedrals with treasuries open to the public are Canterbury, Gloucester, Lincoln, Norwich and York. There are doubtless others too.

lossary of architectural terms

Abacus A flat slab on top of a capital from which an arch springs

Abutment Masonry used to counter the lateral thrust of a vault or a crossing tower. Aisle vaults act as abutments to high vaults (as do flying buttresses), and are themselves supported by external buttresses

Apse Vaulted semi-circular end of a chancel, aisle, or chapel to contain an altar

Arcade A succession of arches on piers or columns

Ashlar Cut, squared masonry, used to face walls.

Bay Repeating unit of an elevation

Capital Bell-shaped piece of masonry surmounting a pier, column, or shaft

Centering Temporary wooden framework used to construct vaults or arches

Clerestory The windowed top storey of the main structure of an aisled building

Corbel Stone projecting from a wall surface to support, or pretend to support, the feature above it

Cusp Projecting point between two foils

Gallery The middle storey of a three-storey elevation opening into the space between the aisle vault and the aisle roof. See also triforium, with which it is often confused

Hammerbeam Horizontal beam projecting from the top of a wall to carry roof braces

Impost Wall-bracket on which the end of an arcade rests

Misericord Projection on the underside of a tip-up seat providing a support for use during standing parts of services

Mullion Vertical stone bar dividing windows into lights

Pendant Elongated boss which gives the impression of hanging from a vault like a stalactite

Pier Free-standing masonry support for arches

Quoins External corner stones

Respond Demi-pier bonded into a wall at the end of an arcade

Soffit The underside of an arch

Spandrel Wall surface between a pair of arches, or the equivalent surface to the side of a single arch

Strainer-arch Arch inserted between verticals to keep them from leaning

Tie-beam Beam connecting two wall-heads to keep them vertical

Transom Horizontal stone bar used to strengthen windows

Triforium Arcaded wall-passage between arcade and clerestory which does not lead into the aisle roof space

Tympanum Space above the lintel of a doorway and below the arch over it

Vault Arched ceiling, usually of stone

    Tunnel or barrel vault Vault of solid masonry without ribs

    Groined vault Intersection of two tunnel vaults of the same section

    Rib vault Vault with a skeleton of ribs, infilled with thin stone; much lighter than a tunnel vault

    Tierceron vault Vault with tiercerons, which go from one of the main springers or the central boss to a point on one of the ridge ribs

    Lierne vault Vault with tiercerons, and liernes, which are ribs which spring from somewhere other than the main springers or the central boss

    Fan vault Vault in which the curved ribs of identical length form concave half-cones

144